The Origins of the First World War

SECOND EDITION

GORDON MARTEL

LONGMAN
LONDON

Addison Wesley Longman Limited
Edinburgh Gate, Harlow
Essex CM20 2JE, England
and Associated Companies throughout the world.

*Published in the United States of America
by Longman Publishing, New York*

First published 1987
Second Edition 1996

ISBN 0 582 28697 2 PPR

British Library Cataloguing-in-Publication Data

A catalogue record for this book is
available from the British Library

Library of Congress Cataloging-in-Publication Data

Martel, Gordon.
  The origins of the First World War / Gordon Martel. -- 2nd ed.
    p. cm. -- (Seminar studies in history)
  Includes bibliographical references and index.
  ISBN 0-582-28697-2
    1. World War, 1914–1918--Causes. 2. Europe--Politics and
  government--1871–1918. I. Title. II. Series.
  D511.M269 1996
  940.3'11--dc20   95-4505
                                                                 CIP

Set by 7 in 10/12 Sabon Roman
Produced through Longman Malaysia, PP

CONTENTS

EDITORIAL FOREWORD

Such is the pace of historical enquiry in the modern world that there is an ever-widening gap between the specialist article or monograph, incorporating the results of current research, and general surveys, which inevitably become out of date. *Seminar Studies in History* are designed to bridge this gap. The books are written by experts in their field who are not only familiar with the latest research but have often contributed to it. They are frequently revised, in order to take account of new information and interpretations. They provide a selection of documents to illustrate major themes and provoke discussion, and also a guide to further reading. Their aim is to clarify complex issues without over-simplifying them, and to stimulate readers into deepening their knowledge and understanding of major themes and topics.

ROGER LOCKYER

NOTE ON REFERENCING SYSTEM

Readers should note that numbers in square brackets [5] refer them to the corresponding entry in the Bibliography at the end of the book (specific page numbers are given in italics). A number in square brackets preceded by *Doc.* [*Doc. 5*] refers readers to the corresponding item in the Documents section which follows the main text. Words which are defined in the Glossary are asterisked on their first occurrence in the book.

LIST OF MAPS

PART ONE: THE PROBLEM

1 THE OUTBREAK OF WAR

On a summer's morning late in June 1914, the heir to the throne of the Habsburg monarchy arrived at the Bosnian town of Sarajevo for an official visit. While the Archduke Franz Ferdinand, his wife and his entourage proceeded through the crowded main street of the city in open motor-cars, a young man stepped out of the crowd and hurled something at the Archduke. A bomb exploded, narrowly missing its target, and the would-be assassin was quickly seized. The Archduke, against the advice of his aides, insisted that they continue their journey to the town hall. Here the Austrians endured a fulsome speech by the mayor, saturated with unintentionally ironic references to the loyalty of the Bosnian people and the esteem in which the Archduke was held in the province. When this agony had ended, Franz Ferdinand insisted that he be permitted to visit the hospital to see one of his aides who had been injured by the exploding bomb. As the party retraced its route along the main street, some confusion occurred, which resulted in the Archduke's chauffeur being forced to stop and reverse direction in the middle of the street. Seizing this unexpected opportunity, another assassin emerged, this time with a pistol rather than a bomb; quickly taking aim, he shot Franz Ferdinand in the throat. Within minutes both the Archduke and his wife lay dead. Before the summer was over, this dramatic event would lead to the greatest war Europe had ever known.

Few Europeans at the time anticipated that the murder of an Austrian archduke would draw them into a crisis and then into a war: assassinations were not unknown in Europe, but few of them had led to armed conflict. The Balkans seemed far away not only to the English, but to the French and to the Germans as well. Europe had weathered much more threatening crises in the recent past, and the first few days following the death of the Archduke were notable mainly for the absence of activity.

Many were surprised by how slowly the Austrians responded to the assassination, which seemed to confirm the impression that the incident at Sarajevo would soon be forgotten. It was widely known that, for various reasons, Franz Ferdinand was not a popular man in court circles in Vienna; nor was there any sign of a popular outcry for revenge among the peoples of Austria-Hungary. But, as is often the case in the course of diplomatic affairs, this tranquil appearance was misleading. Within the Austrian government there was a strong conviction that Serbia was responsible, that this gunman did not act alone, and that he actually enjoyed the unofficial support of the Serbian government. The Austrians quickly discovered that the assassin and his compatriots were Serbian nationalists, members of a terrorist group called the 'Black Hand', whose ambition it was to incorporate all Serbian peoples within the Serbian state. Behind the scenes in Vienna, politicians, diplomats and strategists were hotly debating the question of how far and how fast to move in responding to this outburst of Serbian nationalism. Many Austrian officials regarded the nationalism of minority groups as the greatest threat to the continuing existence of the Habsburg monarchy and they saw in the assassination the perfect opportunity to crush the Serbian-sponsored movement in Bosnia. Although they lacked proof of complicity on the part of the Serbian government, the Austrians, after three weeks of negotiation and debate, agreed to despatch an ultimatum that they believed Serbia could not possibly accept; the terms were designed to end Serbia's existence as a sovereign state. The ultimatum was presented at 6 p.m. on 23 July; the Serbs were given only forty-eight hours to comply.

Two days later, three hours before their reply was due, the Serbian government ordered their army to mobilise. But they also presented a note to the Austrian government written in language that was sufficiently ambiguous to convince some observers that they were, in essence, prepared to accept the terms of the ultimatum. In spite of this uncertainty, the Austrians nevertheless ordered the mobilisation of seven army corps against Serbia. The following day the Russian government, which was prepared to support Serbia against an Austrian attack, decided to undertake a series of steps that would enable them to carry out a full mobilisation, in the event that Serbia's acceptance of the ultimatum did not go far enough to satisfy the Austrians. At 11 a.m. on 28 July, less than five days after presenting the ultimatum, Austria-Hungary declared war on Serbia.

Later on that same day, during the afternoon of 28 July, Russia announced that she too would mobilise – but only in those districts that would enable her to go to war with Austria-Hungary. This partial mobilisation, which was designed to avoid the appearance of threatening Germany, was initiated at midnight, 29 July. But by the following day the Russian government had decided that restricting their mobilisation to their Austro-Hungarian frontier would place them in a perilous position, should Germany come into the conflict. On 30 July Russia ordered a full mobilisation. The possibility of localising the crisis seemed to have evaporated.

Austria-Hungary responded to the Russian decision by ordering a general mobilisation on 31 July. War between the Russians and the Austrians now appeared to be inevitable. Consequently, the German government ordered their army to mobilise and despatched an ultimatum of their own to Russia demanding the immediate cessation of all military measures against Germany and Austria-Hungary within twelve hours. When the Russians failed to reply to this ultimatum, the Germans declared war on them at 6 p.m. on 1 August. The French ordered a general mobilisation on the same day; the Germans declared war on them two days later. On the morning of 4 August German troops crossed the Belgian frontier; by midnight Germany and Great Britain were at war.

The preceding summary is a very superficial one; entire books have been written that cover only the details of these events [79; 109]. Nevertheless, students may still begin to have some sense of the complexities involved in answering the deceptively simple question of 'how did the war begin?' No one, not even the Austrians, went to war for the sake of Franz Ferdinand; and yet a direct line can be drawn between his murder, the diplomatic crisis, the mobilisations and the declarations of war. There was clearly more to the July crisis than meets the eye – more than ultimatums and mobilisations. Why did the Austrians attempt to eliminate Serbia as a sovereign state? Why did the Russians decide to risk war by mobilising in support of the Serbs? How did the Germans become involved in a dispute that apparently had little to do with them? Why did the French decide to mobilise their troops when war broke out in the east? Why did the British choose to go to war for the sake of Belgium? Or did they? And where were the Italians? Although a member of the Triple Alliance for thirty-four years, Italy did not enter the war until 1915.

In order to answer these questions we must unravel the diplomatic ties that connected these events to one another; we must understand what the 'alliance system' was and how it bound – or failed to bind – states to one another. In the aftermath of the First World War, many acute observers insisted that it was the system of alliances that led the states of Europe down the slippery slope to war in July 1914. The impression that once the crisis had been provoked by the assassin's bullets the alliance system took over and rendered diplomats helpless became widespread after 1919. The complicated network of political commitments had led to the creation of intricate mobilisation plans, which eventually led to 'War by TimeTable' – the title of one popular book on the subject [111]. The League of Nations was founded partly on the belief that it could provide an alternative to the security that the alliances had appeared to offer to the states that joined them.

But statesmen seldom act on the basis of simple legal commitments, and even when we unravel the entangling alliances and alignments that tied the states of Europe to one another, we shall only discover another layer of more fundamental – and more profound – questions that require answers if we are to understand how a great European war began in August 1914. The alliances are, in many respects, the easiest subject to explore when studying the origins of the war: they are well-documented; their terms can be analysed; their effectiveness can be measured. But the Italians managed to avoid living up to their promises, while there was nothing on paper that bound the British to the Russians and the French. So what were the 'underlying' causes of the war? What sentiments and emotions, ambitions and fears prepared governments and peoples alike to gamble their existence in 1914 [88; 91]?

Of all the phenomena associated with the outbreak of the war, nationalism is obviously the one that has most fascinated historians. Part of this fascination can be readily explained by the events of July: nationalism was unquestionably the force that propelled the young Serbs of Bosnia into plotting the assassination of Franz Ferdinand [100]; nationalism was unquestionably the phenomenon that the Austrians saw themselves fighting against when they presented their ultimatum [228]; and the feeling of brotherhood based upon a common Slavic identity was unquestionably a factor in leading the Russians to regard themselves as the protectors of the Serbs [267]. But the interest in this phenomenon far exceeds the events of July; almost every historian engaged in writing the history of Europe has identified nationalism as one of the most influential forces that shaped modern history. Or, to put it another way, no historian has argued that the sense of nationality was *not* a factor in the outbreak of war in 1914 [75; 87].

Only slightly less elusive than the idea of nationalism is that of militarism. By the time that the crisis came in July, the continental states of Europe had amassed standing armies of unprecedented size. The conscription of millions of young men by their governments to serve in the armed forces for one, two, or even three years was the rule in pre-war Europe, to which Britain was the exception. This undoubtedly attests to the authority of the modern state, both in terms of the power that it can muster, but also in the sense of being able to insist on the compliance of its citizens. Were the young men of Europe forced to the front against their will in 1914? Or does this phenomenon indicate a popular tide of warlike enthusiasm among the peoples of Europe that overwhelmed the statesmen who were unable to stem the tide of the forces that they had unleashed [61]? Even in Britain, with its tiny professional army, amateur militarism was a popular entertainment before the war [332].

And what was all that marching and drilling supposed to achieve? What were all those symbols of nationality and patriotic zeal supposed to inspire? Did they not all boil down to imperialistic expansionism [198]? The late nineteenth century was the great age of European dominance: Africa had been partitioned; much of Asia was ruled by Europeans; the Ottoman and Chinese empires appeared to be on the verge of collapse. Was the war within Europe really a struggle for spoils beyond it? Did European governments not consciously manipulate their people into supporting their drive to acquire new resources and markets by promoting xenophobia and inspiring war scares [200]? Is it not true that the war within Europe was really a contest to see who would be master outside it [80]?

Nationalism, militarism and imperialism are the most prominent of the 'underlying' causes of war that historians have investigated in their attempts to go beneath the surface of the events that led to war in 1914. Historians began assessing these factors even before the war ended, and they are assessing them still; students who turn to the 'classic' treatments that appeared between the wars in books by Sidney Fay [79] and Bernadotte Schmitt [109] will find these themes clearly being discussed from the beginning. In the more detailed, better documented accounts that appeared after the Second World War in books by William L. Langer [91], A.J.P. Taylor [110], Luigi Albertini [62] and Pierre Rénouvin [104] these themes were not abandoned. It has been apparent from the start that these are the issues that will not go away and that, although it is impossible to assess the relative effect of such elements in some neatly hierarchical manner, it is essential to investigate the factors that altered perceptions, stimulated ambitions and generated fears. Any attempt to explain the origins of the war must take them into account.

One line of investigation not pursued in the English-speaking world until half a century after the outbreak of the war, was the possibility that war arose from the desire on the part of the guardians of the old order to forestall a social conflict at home by engaging in war abroad. This argument was first put forward in Germany by Eckhardt Kehr, a radical young historian who, in a number of essays, argued for *Der Primat der Innenpolitik* ('the primacy of domestic politics'). Kehr's argument that the industrialists and landowners of pre-war Germany combined to prevent domestic reform through a policy of *Sammlungspolitik* ('the politics of rallying together') took hold with a number of influential historians in Germany [145; 217]. This argument was then extended to explain how a crisis, or even a war, would come to be seen by those who were making the decisions to be a more attractive alternative than domestic reform [129; 152]. During the past twenty years historians have applied elements of this thesis to explain the policies of Britain [360], Russia [264] and Italy [243].

It may now be difficult for us to imagine a time and a place in which war was not only acceptable but popular. For students, the greater the gap in time between themselves and their subject, the more difficult it is to recapture the attitudes and the ideas that made up the emotional world in which Europeans lived early in this century. Two world wars, numerous revolutions, a great depression, the advent of atomic weapons and bloody ethnic conflicts separate us psychologically from the men and women of 1914. The kind of thinking that led people to rejoice at the prospect of war is now difficult to recapture – but rejoice they did: there was dancing in the streets and spontaneous demonstrations of support for governments throughout Europe. Men flocked to recruiting offices, fearful that the war might end before they had the opportunity to fight. There was a spirit of festival and a sense of community in all European cities as old class divisions and political rivalries were replaced by patriotic fervour. Students seeking to understand the origins of the First World War must be sensitive to the emotional distance that separates them from their forebears.

But students of history should also understand that distance can be an advantage. The question, 'how did the war begin' was frequently posed immediately after the war, but in a very different political climate. People were then less concerned with the question of how the war began than they were with determining responsibility for it. This quest was particularly passionate in Germany, where it came to be known as the *Kriegschuldfrage** (the 'war guilt question'), a question that arose directly from the Paris Peace Conference of 1919 [126]. There, the 'Commission on the Responsibility of the Authors of the War and on the Enforcement of Penalties' concluded that the responsibility for the outbreak of war 'lies wholly upon the Powers which declared war in pursuance of a policy of aggression'. Not surprisingly, the victorious powers determined that Germany and Austria (together with their allies, Turkey and Bulgaria) had premeditated the war, and had brought it about by acts 'deliberately committed in order to make it unavoidable'.

No doubt this assessment of blame would in itself have aroused wounded feelings within Germany and Austria [141]. But in inter-war Europe there was more than wounded feelings at stake because the victorious Allies went on to justify their demand for reparations on the basis of the Commission's report. So the debate on war origins had a practical as well as an abstract side to it, and the question of war guilt quickly became the most hotly debated historical subject of the 1920s [123]. Those who regarded the Treaty of Versailles as an illegitimate, wicked peace, as a *diktat* imposed upon the vanquished, believed that if they could show that the burden of responsibility rested more with the Allied states than with the Central Powers (or at least that responsibility must be shared equally), then the peace settlement might be revised and a morally defensible system of international relations put in its place [67]. Conversely, those who believed that the power of Germany had to be permanently checked, and that the Austro-Hungarian monarchy was an evil and decadent empire that must give way to nation-states, sought to prove that the Commission was correct to conclude that the Central Powers were responsible for the war [7].

But with the rise of Hitler, the creation of the Third Reich, the outbreak of the Second World War and the horrors of the Holocaust, the controversy over the origins of the First World War steadily lost its hold on the popular imagination. Professional historians continued their investigations of the subject, exploring what seemed to be an endless supply of new documentary evidence, but the subject had lost its punch [76]. Yet in the 1920s, fresh revelations unearthed in the archives or the appearance of new memoirs had been front-page news. Led by Germany, each of the combatants began to compile documentary collections of diplomatic correspondence in the hope that these would demonstrate their innocence. It soon became obvious that no one was innocent. The documents revealed an extremely complicated diplomatic system, a network of alliances and alignments and a variety of conflicting ambitions and fears. These complexities made it increasingly difficult to adhere to the view that any one state was responsible for the war.

If the war-guilt controversy had any result, it was to give the impression that responsibility was somehow shared by all, that all the great powers before 1914 were militaristic and imperialistic, that they all had made secret arrangements to come to the aid of their friends and allies at a moment of crisis, that they all had war plans, mobilisation schedules and railway timetables to adhere to. This conclusion seemed to stand in stark contrast with what was generally assumed to be the truth about the origins of the Second World War, where practically everyone agreed that 'Hitler' was the answer to almost every question that almost anyone might ask about responsibility. Thus, by the 1960s, we had a situation in which the two world wars were treated as discrete subjects: the responsibility for the first was very murky but certainly shared by all; the responsibility for the second was very clear and hardly bore investigation. The only connection drawn between the two was that somehow the brutal, unfair and unjustified terms of the Treaty of Versailles had created an environment in Germany that encouraged the development of Nazism, and that thereby, in some way, the victorious allies of the First World War were ultimately responsible for the Second.

And then came Fritz Fischer, a German historian at the University of Hamburg, whose arguments revived the debate that had lain dormant for more than a generation. When he published *Griff nach der Weltmacht* (the title of which was translated as *Germany's Aims in the First World War*) in 1961, he effectively re-focused attention on Germany. The book was enormously detailed, piling up mountains of evidence to support the argument that Germany had consciously striven to establish itself as a world power in the era before the First World War, a policy that inevitably led first to competition, then to conflict, with Britain and Russia. This seemed to return the argument to where it had been in the 1920s, when the question of Germany's guilt had been primary. But new zest was given to the debate in the 1960s as a result of Fischer's contention that a clear line of continuity could be drawn between the policies of Wilhelmine and Nazi Germany. Suddenly it became possible to argue that German expansionism could be found at the centre of both world wars. In his next book, *Krieg der Illusionen* (War of Illusions) (1969), Fischer went farther still, arguing that the German government had decided to go to war as far back as December

1912, and that the declaration of war had only been postponed until circumstances became more favourable – as they did in July 1914 [217].

Not surprisingly, this argument did not go unchallenged, and soon the origin of the First World War was a hot topic again. Things heated up first in Germany, where historians attacked Fischer from almost every angle: Gerhard Ritter, Karl Dietrich Erdmann, Egmont Zechlin and Erwin Hölzle undertook to discredit Fischer by denouncing him in the press, and they succeeded in persuading the government to cancel a lecture tour of the United States on the grounds that he would tarnish the image of Germany in the eyes of Americans. But Fischer did not find himself alone in the face of this criticism: John Röhl [106], Imanuel Geiss [133; 178], Volker Berghahn [169] and others supported the argument and extended the research upon which it was based. The consequence of all this controversy, as Holger Herwig has argued, is that works on the July crisis published before 1961 are now out of date [204]. They tell us more about the times in which they were written than they do about the subject they are written on, and as such are best treated as a kind of historical archaeology.

The quarter-century that followed the appearance of *Griff nach der Weltmacht* witnessed an explosion of research on the subject of the war's origins, as well as efforts to arrive at a new synthesis [78; 88]. Detailed and sophisticated work based upon painstaking archival investigation has added enormously to both the breadth and the depth of our understanding of pre-war Europe. F.R. Bridge, Richard Bosworth, Keith Wilson, René Girault, Douglas Porch and Wayne Thompson have revealed new complexities in the political, economic and military processes that set the war in motion; complexities that have, in turn, stimulated fresh controversies far removed from the Fischer debate. Important new syntheses have been provided by Zara Steiner, Dominic Lieven, Richard Bosworth and Samuel Williamson in the Macmillan/St Martin's Press series on 'The Making of the 20th Century' – although these have thus far been limited to national perspectives rather than a more generalised, European one.

This book is not designed to provide a new synthesis, but rather to introduce the subject to students by summarising the major themes in a clear and succinct way. Like most stories, the first, and perhaps the most difficult, choice for historians is to decide where to begin. In fact, few choices are more revealing than those first few pages of a book or first few paragraphs of a scholarly article. Historians writing about the origins of the First World War have started their stories at almost every imaginable point; a few have attempted to avoid such a choice by constructing a non-narrative approach.

In spite of the preceding remarks about the fascination with 'underlying' causes, some historians have concentrated their attention on the events of the summer of 1914. Historians who begin here reveal that they do not accept the argument that the war was the inevitable result of underlying forces. They resist the suggestion that war was intrinsic to the nature of the European states system. Instead, they argue that, had it not been for the peculiarities of the July crisis, war might have been avoided. This view places the burden of responsibility on one or more of the men who actually made the decisions that summer: on Count Berchtold, the Austro-Hungarian minister of foreign affairs, because of his determination to crush Serbian independence; on Serge Sazonov, the Russian minister of foreign affairs, because of his decision to support Serbia by attempting a partial mobilisation of Russian forces; on Wilhelm II, the German emperor, because he pushed Austria into taking a hard line in the crisis; on Raymond Poincaré, the French president, because he assured Russia of French support for her policy in the Balkans; and on Sir Edward Grey, the British foreign minister, because he failed to choose between restraining Russia or warning Germany that Britain would fight alongside Russia and France should war break out in eastern Europe. Concentrating on the July crisis does not, therefore, imply that any particular state or statesman was responsible for war, but it does reveal an assumption that this crisis could have been managed successfully, as had others in the past.

Few historians today would choose to focus their attention exclusively on the immediate events that led to war; the most widespread assumption underlying contemporary interpretations of the First World War is that the crisis of July was the logical (if not necessarily the inevitable) culmination of deep-seated antagonisms and fundamental forces [70; 92]. Interest in the July crisis itself has waned: we seem to have reached the point where we know almost everything we are ever going to know about who said what to whom at what moment. But historians have thought this about subjects before and been proved wrong; perhaps the collapse of the Soviet Union and the disintegration of Yugoslavia will produce new revelations.

Students will therefore discover that most narratives begin before the assassination at Sarajevo, and that they take their story at least as far back as 1902–07 and the 'diplomatic revolution' of those years [93; 159]. During this crucial period Great Britain, it is argued, departed from her long-standing policy of 'splendid isolation' during which she remained aloof from the continental alliances. A turning-point was reached when Britain formed an alliance with Japan in 1902. This, it can be argued, led directly to the Russo-Japanese War in February 1904. The conflict between the Russians and the Japanese, by threatening to drag in their respective partners, the British and the French, led directly to the Anglo-French 'entente' in April 1904. The crushing blow that was dealt to the Russian fleet by the Japanese at the Battle of Tsushima led to the Treaty of Portsmouth in September 1905, which signified the rise of Japan and the descent of Russia. This, in turn, led the Russians to give up their imperialist, expansionist designs in both the far east and in central Asia, thus making possible the 'entente' with the British of August 1907. But a focus on the events of these three years usually indicates the belief that they reveal a fundamental change in British attitudes – a change that can be interpreted as either an imperialist plot designed to encircle Germany or as a defensive response to the threat of German expansionism in Africa, the Middle East and Asia.

In fact, German expansionism has also been the focus of some who examine these years in particular detail [169; 180]. Germany, they argue, had been undergoing a profound transformation since 1870, but it was not until this period that these changes came to be reflected in her foreign policy. Following the turn of the century she adopted a 'world policy' which reflected her determination to break out from the difficult position of being located in central Europe at a time of world-wide expansion on the part of other great powers – a determination that was symbolised by her decision to build an ocean-going battle fleet. The challenge confronting her in these years, declared the chancellor, Prince Bernhard von Bülow, was whether Germany was going to be 'the hammer' or 'the anvil' of world politics [*Doc. 2*]. The Moroccan crisis of 1905 was the direct result of this line of thinking within Germany. When Germany failed to secure the diplomatic victory she sought at the Algeciras Conference in 1906, she concentrated on challenging Britain at sea by escalating her naval building programme. Historians who concentrate on the years 1902–07, by focusing attention on the Anglo-Japanese alliance, the Anglo-French entente, the first Moroccan crisis, the naval race and the Anglo-Russian entente, usually reveal a belief that the First World War was fundamentally an Anglo-German confrontation, a competition for empire outside Europe.

Other historians see the war not as an imperialist confrontation over resources and opportunities outside Europe, but as the inescapable conflict between the two great alliance systems on the European continent. The roots of this system lay in Europe, and particularly in eastern Europe. Consequently, they begin their story in the period 1879–94. In 1879 the Dual Alliance of Austria and Germany was established, a defensive arrangement in which each of them promised to assist the other if either were attacked by Russia; or to provide assistance in the case of an attack on one of them in which Russia actively co-operated or in which she undertook 'menacing' military measures [*Doc. 1*]. When Italy joined Austria and Germany three years later the arrangement was transformed into the Triple Alliance. As long as Bismarck was around to guide the alliance, and as long as he was able to remain on good terms with Russia, it seems – at least to most historians – to have posed little danger to peace, and perhaps to have done a great deal to maintain it [181].

When Wilhelm II ascended the throne in 1888, however, a *neue Kurs** ('new course') was initiated in German foreign policy, which soon led to the dismissal of Bismarck and the end of Russo-German harmony. The new kaiser, only twenty-nine years old, looked upon the old chancellor (seventy-three years old) as too conservative for the new Germany. If the only way for Germany to expand her power and her prestige meant offending Russia, then so be it. The result was that Russia, determined not to yield her position of dominance in south-eastern Europe, chose to align herself with France through a political agreement in August 1891, a military convention in August 1892 and an alliance in January 1894. France, determined to take advantage of the Russo-German rift, saw an opportunity to perhaps avenge her defeat at the hands of Prussia in 1870–71, and by 1894 a formal Franco-Russian alliance had been established [*Doc. 7*]. Henceforth Europe was starkly divided into two armed camps, and a spark, falling in the right place, could set off a European conflagration at any moment. The 'alliance system' has, in itself, often been regarded as a cause of the First World War, almost apart from the policies that gave rise to its creation.

More direct responsibility is proposed by those who begin their account in 1870–71, which is regarded as a decisive turning-point because of the dramatic victory of Prussia over France. Those who see the First World War arising logically from the growth of German power – and not from the ambitions of Wilhelm II and his militarist and navalist advisers – are naturally inclined to interpret the creation of the German empire in 1871 as the proper starting-point for their account [201; 202]. The astonishing speed with which France, hitherto regarded as the greatest of European powers, was soundly defeated by Prussia, indicated that the new German state might soon be in a position to dominate the continent.

But it is possible to see in 1870–71 a turning-point that focuses attention on France rather than Germany. In this view France, humiliated by her defeat and deprived of Alsace-Lorraine by the Treaty of Frankfurt, followed a policy of *revanche** ('revenge') that would lead to another war with Germany as soon as she felt herself strong enough to win. And a key to this feeling would be an arrangement with Russia that would enable France to avoid the isolation in which she had found herself in 1870. Thus, historians who begin their story in 1870–71 are inclined to regard either Germany or France as the state primarily responsible for war in 1914, although they may also attribute it to the more general breakdown in the balance of power that had kept Europe relatively peaceful since 1815 [102; 103].

The farther back in time historians go in tracing the story of origins, the more likely it is that they see general, underlying causes as the proper explanation of the war: particular personalities and specific events fade against a more illuminating background. Some, for example, choose 1848 as a focal point: the crushing of liberal revolutions in central and eastern Europe bolstered the power of despotic, reactionary regimes in Prussia, Russia and Austria-Hungary. This created a Europe in which militarism and authoritarianism triumphed in the centre and the east, which in turn compelled the liberal, parliamentary regimes of western Europe to defend themselves against their ideological enemies. Others go back as far as 1815 and the Congress of Vienna, where the conservative statesmen responsible for the settlement of Europe after the Napoleonic wars attempted to turn the tide of history and repress the legitimate demand of nationalities to form independent states of their own. Most of the international problems in Europe over the following century were caused by nations 'struggling to be free'. This never-ending succession of crises and conflicts could not be localised forever: one of them would inevitably lead to a general conflict. The feeling that Europe was headed for 'Armageddon' grew more persistent throughout the nineteenth century.

There are others who would argue that none of the above approaches are sufficient, that they are all much too limited in their focus. 'Megahistorians' insist that it is necessary to go much further back. Studies such as Oswald Spengler's *Decline of the West* and Arnold Toynbee's *A Study of History*, which were particularly popular in the period between the wars, argue that the First World War was symptomatic of the decline, or the end, of western civilisation itself [150]. They, and others, see Europe slowly heading for disaster since the Reformation, when religious sectarianism shattered the unity of Christendom and led to independent states with conflicting identities; or since the Renaissance, which eroded the spiritual foundations of the West by promoting secular humanism; or since the fall of the Roman Empire, which eliminated the only structure capable of keeping the peace over such a large and variegated variety of peoples; or since the triumph of rationalism in Greece, which replaced a peaceful, matriarchal culture with a warlike, masculine one [150].

Like all accounts of the First World War, this one must begin somewhere, and no doubt my choices will reveal something of my own assumptions and prejudices. But I have made an effort to minimise my own views and interpretations; my purpose has been to provide as clear and as succinct a summary of the origins of the First World War as I can. I have chosen to begin with an account of the great powers up to 1900. I have divided the chapters along the lines by which the powers were themselves divided by that time: Germany, Austria-Hungary and Italy within the Triple Alliance, France and Russia within the Dual Alliance, and Great Britain standing on the periphery. I have then attempted to sketch the broad outlines of the foreign policy pursued by each of the states throughout the nineteenth century, the changes that occurred in the second half of the century, and how these changes led to the creation of the alliance system and to alterations in what is usually referred to as the 'Balance of Power'. In attempting to produce this sketch I have made an effort to pay special attention to the question of how internal structures influenced the direction of foreign policy in each of the great powers – a subject that has preoccupied many historians for the past quarter-century. Once I have portrayed the state of affairs that existed in 1900, I have then followed the course of events, the diplomatic rearrangements, crises and wars that led up to the July crisis, and finally to war.

PART TWO: THE GREAT POWERS TO 1900

2 THE TRIPLE ALLIANCE

The stability of an international system will break down when the growing power of one state destroys the old network of relationships upon which the system was based. In this sense, a state that expands its power through a growth in population, trade, prosperity, industry or territory may be responsible for the breakdown of a system, even if it is not guilty of it. Specialists in the study of international relations refer to this perspective as the 'systemic' level of analysis, in which the whole system is taken into account when attempting to explain why certain events occurred [85; 105]. More important than the policies or the personalities of any given state or its leaders are shifts in the foundations of power, to which governments and statesmen are simply forced to respond.

The breakdown of a system does not make a great war inevitable; it does, however, make war more likely as the states that derived benefits from the old system calculate that it is worth the risk of defeat on the battlefield to prevent the establishment of a new system. Therefore, it is important when considering the origins of any great war to determine which states were expanding the base of their power, and which states felt threatened by such a change. It is also worth considering whether or not the state whose power is growing is conscious of the need to create a new pattern of relations, whether there is a sense that without a change in this pattern it will not be permitted to continue to grow, or that it will be prevented from enjoying the benefits of its growth.

There is no doubt that Germany was the most dynamic state within the European system in the half-century leading up to 1914. This is perhaps the one point on which all historians are agreed. Those who lived through the decades leading up to the First World War found it difficult to assess the changing nature of growing states outside Europe: the United States and Japan were puzzling to them, and few believed that these two states were worth analysing in any detail, as their conditions seemed too far removed from those of Europe for useful lessons to be learned. Nor, in the case of the

United States and Japan, was it believed that they could ever have much impact upon the European system. But Germany was another matter. No state was more closely watched than Germany after 1870. Anyone interested in military power, in politics, in economic change, felt that they must take the German example into account – if only to criticise and respond to it. Everyone believed that they could learn from the German example, and German thought, literature and music enjoyed an unprecedented popularity outside Germany. In the years following the wars of unification, the assumption that Germany was capable of upsetting the foundations upon which the international system was built began to spread throughout Europe. The focus of international attention, hitherto located in Paris, shifted to Berlin; Bismarck became the most important statesman in the world.

The three wars that Prussia fought to create the new German empire – against Denmark in 1864, against Austria in 1866, and against France in 1870 – demonstrated her military prowess. No one was really surprised when Prussia, in alliance with Austria, defeated Denmark. But the speed and the ease with which Austria was defeated two years later startled observers, who had expected a relatively balanced conflict; and Prussia's victory in the war with France four years later was even more astonishing. Even in the 1860s France had been regarded both as the greatest power in continental Europe and as the state most inclined – by tradition and by ideology – to destroy the European system that had been in place since 1815. Her quick and overwhelming defeat at the hands of Prussia decisively altered everyone's appreciation of the foundations of European relations. Germany would now make things happen; henceforth others would respond to her initiatives.

Prussia's victories were also important because they taught a political lesson that was keenly appreciated by statesmen and students of politics alike: that defeat in war was likely to bring about fundamental changes within the state that lost on the battlefield. Austria's defeat led to the *Ausgleich** ('compromise') of 1867 in which the Germans of the Habsburg empire were forced to share power with the Hungarians. France's defeat led to the destruction of the Second Empire and to the formation of the Third Republic in 1871 [97]. Henceforth, those who might be prepared to embark on a policy of adventure would have to weigh more carefully their prospects, because defeat in war could quite possibly lead to the disappearance of the political system for which they were fighting. Ironically, the revolution in the international system caused by the formation of a powerful new German empire simultaneously produced an atmosphere of caution and conservatism.

The new Germany could very easily have come to be regarded as a revolutionary power, as a state prepared to overturn the established international order and to foment radical political change. But this was a role that Germany's chancellor, Prince Otto von Bismarck, was determined not to play. In spite of Germany's tremendous victories, he believed that the new empire faced immediate danger as a result of having defeated two of her three great neighbours. If Germany did not now behave cautiously, she could easily encourage the formation of a coalition of France, Austria-Hungary and Russia, whose combined power would be too much for her to match. Bismarck believed that he had succeeded in unifying Germany only because he had managed to isolate first Denmark, then Austria, and finally France. As strong as the new Germany was, she was in no position to fight a war on three fronts, and Bismarck believed that he needed time to consolidate the new empire. This meant upholding the *status quo*, thereby guaranteeing Germany's neighbours that she had no further ambitions to pursue that would endanger their security or their political systems [171]. Bismarck the revolutionary was transformed into Bismarck the conservative statesman.

The method by which Bismarck chose to protect the new empire from the revenge of her neighbours was a system of alliances. He began with the assumption that it would be impossible to make a friend of France. Therefore, by the terms of the Treaty of Frankfurt, which ended the Franco-Prussian War, he did his best to ensure that France would be in no position to undertake an offensive campaign against Germany. The large indemnity, on which he insisted, would throw France's finances into chaos and consequently deprive her of the funds necessary to fight a great war. Furthermore, the annexation of Alsace and Lorraine would deprive France of rich territory and the most promising ground from which to attack Germany [102]. Neither of these provisions would, however, prevent France from undertaking a war of revenge if she thought that she could find the allies necessary to involve Germany in a two-front or three-front war. France, therefore, must be deprived of the allies she required for such a design. Bismarck concentrated his efforts on Austria-Hungary and Russia.

At first, these efforts amounted to no more than vague declarations of friendship expressed by the Hohenzollern, Habsburg and Romanov emperors of Germany, Austria-Hungary and Russia when Bismarck succeeded in bringing them together in 1872–73. Although this *Dreikaiserbund** ('League of the Three Emperors') was far from an alliance, it was nevertheless an important achievement for Bismarck because it publicised the fact that the rulers of Austria-Hungary and Russia did not regard Germany as an international criminal. Moreover, by emphasising the monarchical ties that bound together the ruling families of central and eastern Europe, Bismarck attained one of his ambitions: to make republican France appear to be the entity that threatened the stability of existing regimes in Europe.

Bismarck's satisfaction with his achievement was short-lived. He soon recognised that the French had recovered from the war more quickly than he had anticipated; a great outpouring of patriotic sentiment enabled the French to pay off the indemnity more quickly than anyone had believed possible. The next logical step in his programme was to attempt to deprive France of her most likely ally by offering Austria-Hungary an alliance with Germany. While the French might be able to hold out the possibility of a war that could lead to the dismantling of the new German empire, Bismarck was able to offer something that they could not: a guarantee against attack by Russia. The Austrians, who proved to be more fearful of the prospect of such an attack than they were hopeful of reversing the decision of 1866, signed an agreement with Germany in 1879 [*Doc. 1*]. Few would have guessed at the time that the Austro-German alliance would become the most enduring political arrangement between the great powers, remaining in effect for almost forty years. When it disappeared, so did the Habsburg and the Hohenzollern empires.

Bismarck had no intention of going to war with Russia in order to preserve Austria-Hungary. He always believed that the key to Germany's security was good relations with Russia, and he sought to ensure these by drawing Russia into a renewed *Dreikaiserbund* in 1881 [181]. The unspoken assumption in this arrangement was that both Russia and Austria-Hungary would forgo the adventurous expansionism in south-eastern Europe that was bound to lead them into conflict; and Bismarck, in order to preserve this state of affairs, would act as the 'honest broker' in disputes between the two empires. The final piece of the puzzle was put into place when Italy joined Germany and Austria-Hungary in the Triple Alliance of 1882 [*Doc. 2*].

The Bismarckian system of alliances was a complicated series of checks and balances, but it achieved two essential objects: it effectively deprived France of any continental ally and it established the German empire as a responsible and respectable state eager to uphold the new *status quo*. These limited aims and the desire for respectability reflected the conservative nature of the new empire, which was, in essence, a coalition of the Prussian monarchy and large landowners [*Doc. 3*]. These conservative elements had, ultimately, been willing to fight the wars of unification only because Bismarck had persuaded them that they were acting defensively, and that the alternative to his policy was unification from below, led by social revolutionaries. The new state, although it did contain some representative institutions, retained the essential ingredients of the old monarchy, leaving great authority in the hands of the kaiser, especially when it came to the making of foreign and defence policy [174].

As eager as the conservatives were to contain social revolution and preserve the old order, the new empire soon began to develop in such a way as to make this difficult to achieve. Industry, which began to grow quickly, stimulated the development of the middle class, which was likely in the future to support liberal ideas of constitutional reform, and of the working class, which was likely in the future to support socialist ideas of revolutionary social change. Both of these forces appeared unsympathetic to the old order. Economic development was making the new Germany less rural and more urban, whereas the political hierarchy was based upon the old agricultural system. The territories of southern Germany, recently incorporated within the empire, were richer, more industrial, more densely populated and more democratic than Prussia. In spite of Bismarck's achievements, therefore, Germany's ruling classes felt that there was a latent internal crisis unfolding within the empire as the new classes created by the industrial revolution came to challenge the basis of the Prusso-German system established in 1871 [197; 200].

Ironically, this fear of a latent crisis ran parallel to a growing sense of power – a confusing impression of reality that existed most conspicuously in the mind of Wilhelm II, who became kaiser in July 1888. Throughout his reign, which lasted until 1918, Wilhelm was torn between his fears of a social revolution and his ambitions to see Germany become a world power. By the time he acceded to the throne, Germany was the second most populous nation in Europe (after Russia); she produced more coal, more iron and more steel than any other nation on the continent. The kaiser believed that Germany's new power made it possible for her to break free from Bismarck's cautious preservation of the *status quo*, for which he had relied particularly on the conservative friendship with Russia. Wilhelm II was not interested in continuing to play the role of 'honest broker' in disputes between the Austrians and the Russians in the near east. By forcing Bismarck's resignation in 1890, he launched Germany upon a bold *Neue Kurs* in foreign policy. Germany herself had interests to develop in south-eastern Europe and in the middle east, which Wilhelm symbolised by visiting the sultan in Constantinople in 1889 – a stark contrast to Bismarck's earlier declaration that the Balkans were not worth 'the bones of a Pomeranian grenadier'. Germany's ambitions could best be developed by strengthening the alliance with Austria and ceasing to worry about the possible repercussions from Russia [186; 193]. Wilhelm gave his personal assurance to Franz Joseph, the Habsburg emperor, that in any crisis Germany would mobilise her forces simultaneously with Austria, no matter what the issue; he declined to renew the Reinsurance Treaty of 1887 with Russia in which the two states had promised not to attack one another [*Doc. 4*]. The shift from a balanced, tripartite arrangement to one in which Germany was increasingly committed to Austria-Hungary was readily apparent to all observers.

The new course in German policy was undoubtedly instrumental in prompting the Russians to consider seriously the French suggestions for an alliance; within a year the French fleet visited Kronstadt; within two years France and Russia constructed a military agreement. Rather than destroying the principles upon which the *neue Kurs* was founded, however, this new development in European politics merely served to confirm them. The kaiser had accepted the arguments of his general staff that Germany's military might had now reached a level that made it possible to contemplate fighting a war on two fronts, but that such a scenario made it essential for Germany to have an indivisible alliance with Austria-Hungary and an understanding with Great Britain. In the summer of 1892 General Schlieffen, the new chief of the general staff, argued that, as a two-front war was now inevitable, Germany had to plan accordingly. As a quick defeat of Russia would be difficult (if not impossible) he proposed to attack France first, defeating her quickly and decisively while remaining on the defensive against Russia in the east. The Schlieffen plan* guaranteed that any crisis that led to war with Russia would also lead to a German offensive against France [188].

Schlieffen's strategy required a much larger army, and he got one in July 1893. But there the expansion of the army stopped. By 1900 the German army was no larger than the French, and 300,000 men smaller than the Russian. After the First World War most of the German military blamed the politicians for permitting this relative deterioration of the army to occur. In fact, although Schlieffen himself always advocated an increase in numbers, his colleagues did not, and ultimately the freeze on the size of the army was according to the general staff's own policies, which were grounded in their fear of a social revolution. Further expansion of the army would have required the admission of 'bourgeois' elements into the officer corps, which would dilute the social exclusiveness of the corps – currently consisting of the landowning classes – and propagate the liberal, democratic ideals popular among the middle class. Furthermore, an expansion in the number of conscripts would mean drawing in more men from the urban proletariat, many of whom would be infected with dangerous ideas of socialism. These fears would have counted for less had there not been a widespread expectation of an impending social conflict in which the army alone could safeguard the monarchical-landowner state; if the troops were socialists, or if they were commanded by liberals, the army might prove unwilling to act against revolutionaries in the future [213; 183].

Germany's diplomacy reflected this awkward combination of strength and weakness. Her policy was predicated upon the assumption that she was strong enough to fight a two-front war, but too weak internally to go on increasing her army to match those of France and Russia [Doc. 8]. Wilhelm II and his advisers repeatedly resisted opportunities to abandon the principles of the new course, preferring instead to bolster it by means of closer connections with Austria-Hungary, Britain and Italy. They were increasingly dependent on the Austrians who, if they broke away from the alliance, would destroy the keystone of the new course. Britain and Italy were important in this respect: if Austria-Hungary could be certain that, in the event of a war with Russia, Italy would not attack her in the south, and that Britain would neutralise Russia at the Straits and in the Black Sea, then she would be more inclined to remain committed to her alliance with Germany. Because Italy was competing with France for empire in the Mediterranean, it did not seem difficult to keep her within the fold of the Triple Alliance. Britain proved more difficult to persuade [178].

Wilhelm II favoured a closer understanding with Great Britain from the beginning of his reign. If Germany's future lay in the middle east, through south-eastern Europe, Russia was clearly marked as her main competitor. As Anglo-Russian antagonism had been the most consistent element in international relations since the War of Greek Independence in the late 1820s, it seemed reasonable to assume that the British would be happy to join an anti-Russian coalition. Even with the French alliance, Russia would not be in a position to withstand the combined efforts of Germany, Austria-Hungary and Britain along her eastern and southern frontiers. This arrangement would be so advantageous to the British, who must recognise the inevitability of an Anglo-Russian war over the future of Asia, that they should be prepared to make concessions to the Germans outside Europe. Such co-operation would symbolise the success of the new course [190; 209].

The British, however, refused throughout the 1890s to be drawn into the alliance, and the Germans gradually became convinced that the British would be persuaded to join only if the consequences of remaining aloof became too dangerous [148]. Herein lies the diplomatic origin of the 'risk fleet': Germany could build a naval force strong enough to ensure that Britain would not dare run the risk of war with her [168; 189]. This would draw the British into the alliance and encourage friendly behaviour in Asia and Africa, where territorial concessions would provide the German government with examples of the success of its foreign policy. A fleet-building programme offered another political advantage inside Germany, by holding out to businessmen engaged in heavy industry the promise of reliable, long-term profits through the increasing demand for iron and steel. In this way the monarchical state might be able to rely upon the support of industrialists as well as landowners [173; 191].

By 1900, therefore, Germany had maintained, and even extended, the principles underlying the new course in foreign policy that had begun with the accession of Wilhelm II. She had reaffirmed her commitment to Austria-Hungary, developed war plans based on the assumption of a two-front war, and increased her interests in the near east and in colonial expansion [170]. Germany was the most dynamic element in the international system, and most of her leaders were convinced that they were at a cross-roads: one road led to world power and empire, the other to the minor status of a relatively small state in the centre of Europe [172]. The question facing Germany, as Bernhard von Bülow, the chancellor in 1900, would soon put it, was whether or not she would become 'the hammer or the anvil' of world politics [*Doc. 8*].

The alliance formed between Austria-Hungary and Germany in 1879 ought to be regarded as one of the most surprising events in modern diplomatic history. It is certainly a mistake to assume that the sharing of German language and culture somehow drew the two states together into some close political connection. In fact, throughout the first half of the nineteenth century, nationality did much more to divide the two empires than it did to unite them. The Habsburg rulers of Austria (subsequently Austria-Hungary) recognised that any promotion of the idea of nationality as the principle upon which states should be erected would doom their empire to extinction, and no one saw this more clearly than Count Clemens von Metternich, the leading conservative statesman in Europe from 1815 to 1848. Metternich defined the spirit of diplomacy between the Congress of Vienna and the revolutions of 1848 in much the same way that Bismarck did between the Schleswig-Holstein crisis and the accession of Wilhelm II.

The Habsburg empire owed its creation to traditional dynastic practice; it was an empire made by marriage and inheritance, wars and diplomacy, and it is best thought of as a loose agglomeration of Habsburg 'lands' – an interconnected series of properties belonging to the ruling family – not as a 'nation-state'. Although the Habsburg family and the ruling elite around them was German, the empire, by 1815, included Hungarians, Magyars*, Poles, Czechs, Slovaks, Rumanians, Croatians, Serbs and Italians. The empire may have been a state ruled by Germans, but it did not regard itself as a German state. Moreover, the Germans of the Habsburg empire were overwhelmingly Roman Catholic, which set them apart from the mainly Lutheran Germans of the German empire.

Metternich was especially anxious in the years following the Congress of Vienna to prevent the idea of a 'German nation' from spreading. When Napoleon had cobbled together a series of petty principalities, fiefdoms and bishoprics in southern Germany into what he had called the 'Confederation of the Rhine', he provided further impetus to the idea being broadcast by philosophers like Herder and Fichte that the German people ought to be brought together within a single state. These territories remained linked to one another after 1815 in the new German Confederation* to achieve the very practical purpose of providing what strategists hoped would be a more successful barrier against renewed French expansion than the old, disorganised German states had been. But the Confederation, designed for practical purposes, was soon fulfilling an ideological one: it became the seed-bed of liberal nationalism. Groups of university students, *Burschenschaften*, were particularly active, thus attracting the attention of Metternich who undertook to quash their movement. In other words, the Habsburgs were determined not only to avoid leading the unification of the German people, but to prevent it altogether [224].

Habsburg policy following 1815, therefore, was guided by a reasonably coherent and consistent set of conservative ideas. Metternich supported or proposed various interventions on the part of European governments to put down liberal and nationalist revolts in Spain, Italy and Greece, on the assumption that, if the principle of representative, constitutional, nationalist regimes took root along the frontiers of the empire, it would be only a matter of time before the contagion spread within the empire itself. Italian nationalism was particularly worrying in this respect. The settlement of 1815 had awarded Lombardy and Venetia, the two most prosperous and highly developed territories of the Italian peninsula, to the Habsburgs. Once again, the object was strategic: to provide the Austrians with a more defensible frontier against a renewed French bid for hegemony. The rest of Italy was to remain divided: the kingdom of Sardinia, Parma, Modena, the Papal States, Tuscany and the kingdom of the Two Sicilies provided the Habsburgs with a feeling of security on their southern frontier. As long as these political divisions existed, the Italians would be in no position to pose a threat. If, on the other hand, the Italians demanded, and achieved, the unification of Italian-speaking peoples, this would simultaneously deprive the empire of two rich provinces and leave her vulnerable to attack from the south. Although the prospect of successful revolution caused Metternich to flee Vienna in 1848, his system survived the challenge. As late as 1860, the empire was surrounded, on three sides, by a succession of rather weak states: Bavaria, Saxony and Switzerland to the west; Sardinia, Parma, Modena and the Papal States to the south; the essentially autonomous Ottoman provinces of Bosnia, Serbia, Wallachia and Moldavia to the south and east. The only states in a position to place the Habsburg empire in jeopardy were Prussia and Russia, to the north and north-east. It is hardly surprising then that nationalism, especially of the German and Italian varieties, was perceived to be the main threat to this happy state of affairs [196; 235].

The glaring exception to this strategically beneficial situation was in the east, where there loomed the enormous potential of the Russian empire. The main reason why Metternich had, in the 1820s, gone along with Tsar Alexander I's rather muddle-headed proposal of a 'Holy Alliance' of Christian princes was his desire that Russia should firmly adhere to the principle of monarchical solidarity. The Holy Alliance* became, in effect, a loose association of the Habsburg, Romanov and Hohenzollern rulers to uphold the settlement of 1815 in the face of nationalist and liberal pressures.

The Greek revolt of 1828 opened a fissure between Austria and Russia that never closed, and which foreshadowed the future of their relationship in south-eastern Europe. When the tsar decided, on the grounds of religious principle, to support the demands of the Orthodox Greeks for independence from the Muslim Turks, Metternich objected. He preferred to treat the sultan as a respectable monarch and as a necessary component of the international system: legal sovereignty and political authority were more important than religious identities and linguistic affiliations. Support for Greek independence might well unleash similar demands on the part of other subject peoples – Serbs, Bulgars, Rumanians – in the near east, some of whom were to be found in the Habsburg empire. Moreover, if the rather weak and remote Turkish regime were to disappear from the Balkans and to be replaced with Russian-sponsored regimes, the Habsburg empire would become much more difficult to defend. This underlying fear for the future of the Balkans proved to be one of the most dominant features in the pattern of international relations throughout the nineteenth century [225].

The fissure in the Holy Alliance was closed, temporarily, as a result of the revolutions of 1848. The Habsburg empire was nearly blown to pieces: violence erupted in almost every city, and in Milan, Prague and Budapest nationalist forces seized control, with Italians, Czechs and Hungarians leading the demand for independence or autonomy. The Italians and the Czechs were suppressed only when the army resorted to the most brutal measures. But the strength of the army was not sufficient to suppress the Magyars of Hungary, who were defeated only when the tsar dispatched a force of some 200,000 men to assist his fellow monarch. Russia, in contrast, remained quiet, practically immune to the upheavals of the year of revolution. The conclusion seemed to be that the Habsburg empire was going to find it very difficult to survive in the face of these disintegrative pressures, and that she would have to learn to rely more and more on the Russians propping her up.

The behaviour of Austria during the Crimean War therefore came as a shock to Russia. The Russians assumed, after 1848, that the Habsburg empire was both weak and friendly. She proved to be neither. Austria, rather than supporting Russia in her war with Britain and France, chose to exploit the advantages of the situation in which she found herself: she insisted that Russia must withdraw her forces from the principalities of Wallachia and Moldavia, otherwise Austria would join Britain and France. The Crimean War thus provided the Austrians with the opportunity of barricading the Balkans from further Russian adventures: the principalities were given their independence and re-named Rumania; Russian troops were not to be permitted to advance through them to Constantinople. With the revolutionaries of 1848 either in prison or in exile, and with the Balkans cut off from Russia, Austria appeared, by 1856, to be in a much safer position than she had ten years previously.

But the failure of the revolutions of 1848 convinced many nationalists in the small states of Italy and Germany that they would never be successfully united from below, that it would take war and the connivance of one or two great powers to create a unified state. In the Italian case, this meant that the kingdom of Piedmont-Sardinia had to fight the Austrians for control of Lombardy and Venetia, and, if she were to succeed in this fight, she needed the active co-operation of France [118]. This story is a particularly complicated one, but the result was that Austria was defeated in battle, lost the two provinces, and ceased to be an 'Italian' power. There remained, however, a distinctive Italian population in the Tyrol, which could prove a focal point of future Austro-Italian disputes [120].

Within three years the Habsburgs had also ceased to be a 'German' power. The war with Prussia in 1866, which Bismarck adroitly manoeuvred the Austrians into starting, was really a struggle for the future of Germany; it was to decide whether the German states were to be united under the aegis of Prussia, or whether they would remain a loose association of independent entities, informally presided over by Austria. Defeat on the battlefield was quick, decisive and final, and after 1866 it was clear that Austria was no longer in a position to compete with Prussia as an equal. Bismarck's moderate peace terms (in contrast with the terms imposed on France five years later) reflected the real purpose of the war: the German Confederation was to be dissolved and Austria was to be excluded from German affairs. If Austria were to seek revenge, therefore, it would not be to recover national territory or to relieve the burden of harsh financial and military terms. A war of revenge would mean that Austria had decided to renew the fight to establish her predominance within Germany.

The perfect opportunity for a war of revenge came in 1870 when Prussia went to war with France. But the Austrians did not take advantage of the opportunity; instead, they stood by and waited to see if the French could succeed in turning back the Prussians on their own. There was always the chance that France could, in essence, win Austria's battle for her: if Prussia were soundly defeated, her newly established predominance in the German states of the old confederation would surely evaporate. When this possibility was destroyed on the battlefield, so were any remaining Austrian dreams of recovering her influence in Germany [228]. Austria's acceptance of the new German empire as an irreversible feature of European politics constituted one of the essential foundations of international relations between 1871 and 1914.

The events of 1866–70 had thus caused a profound re-evaluation of Austria's position in Europe; they also caused Austria to be transformed into 'Austria-Hungary', henceforth referred to as the 'Dual Monarchy'*. Following the loss of Lombardy to Piedmont in 1859, the emperor had attempted to strengthen the empire by creating a representative assembly, the Reichsrat*. This reform failed to satisfy the leading nationalities of the empire, however: the Magyars, Italians and Croatians boycotted it; the Czechs, Poles, Serbs and Slovenians opposed it; the new assembly proved unworkable and was held partly responsible for the military failure of 1866. The following year a new system was introduced, a compromise (*Ausgleich*) that transformed the empire into an association of two autonomous states, Austria and Hungary, which were to share the Habsburg emperor as their head of state. They were to have a common foreign policy, defence and finances, and a unique – and cumbersome – process was created to accomplish this. Every ten years the two states were to agree on the expenses necessary to sustain their common foreign policy and defence; the ministers of foreign affairs, defence and finance were to be jointly appointed to both states, and these ministers were to meet once a year with the 'Delegations' (executive committees) drawn from each of the two parliaments, which communicated with one another only in writing. The system of 1867, which was untidy and invited dispute, was manageable only because the cabinet was not responsible to parliament, but to the emperor, and because emergency decrees provided that a cabinet could govern for some time without the support of the legislature [220].

The hope of accommodating the Magyars of Hungary to the empire was the primary objective of these new constitutional arrangements. Austrian strategists believed that the threat of a renewed revolution in Hungary had forced them to fight with a severe handicap against the Italians in 1859 and against the Prussians in 1866. But permitting the Magyars to take the place of equals within the empire inevitably led to some fundamental changes in policy. The Magyars were not interested in the states of western and northern Germany and they were unwilling to make any sacrifices for the recovery of the monarchy's position there. This made an improvement in relations with the new German empire much easier to achieve after 1867. On the other hand, the Magyars and the Germans alike were sensitive to the fact that almost one-half of the people of the empire were Slavic, which led them to fear that the spread of panslavism would lead to the dismemberment of the newly constituted Dual Monarchy. Given these attitudes, it is not surprising that the earlier tendency of Austria to see Russia as an enemy was confirmed, while the defeat at the hands of Prussia was soon forgotten or overlooked.

The alliance with Germany that was signed in 1879 was the logical culmination of this new direction in the policy of Austria-Hungary [*Doc. 1*]. An alliance with a strong Germany now seemed to offer the best protection against Russia. Once Russia was defined as the principal threat to the Dual Monarchy, Austria-Hungary became anxious to expand her alliance with Germany to include Italy. The Austrians had been compelled, when fighting the Prussians in 1866, to keep a large army in the south; although they had defeated the Piedmontese forces at the second battle of Custoza (see Map 2 on p. 137), their ability to defend themselves against the Prussians had been seriously hindered, and they were forced to cede most of Venetia to a united Italy in 1866 [221; 227]. As the same dilemma would almost certainly confront them if they ever went to war with Russia, the Austrians were eager to ensure that their southern frontier would not need to be defended. If, by means of the Triple Alliance, Italian ambitions could be turned in the direction of France and the Mediterranean, the Italian population of the Dual Monarchy was less likely to prove troublesome. Italy was welcomed into the alliance in 1882 [*Doc. 2*].

Austrian foreign policy had, since the Congress of Vienna, been a tangle of complicated and often conflicting interests in Germany, Italy and on the eastern frontier; now it became unusually simple and straightforward. The aim of the Dual Monarchy was to protect itself from disintegrating through the pressures being placed upon it by the forces of panslavism and Balkan nationalism. Austria-Hungary thus became the leading supporter of the *status quo* in the middle east – a policy that culminated in two 'Mediterranean' agreements with Italy and Britain in February/March and December of 1887. The Austrians were as eager as the Germans and the Italians to draw Britain into the Triple Alliance, but by 1896, after repeated refusals on the part of Britain, the Austrians came to believe that they were running too many risks for too little and they declined to renew the Mediterranean agreement. In its place they substituted an arrangement with Russia in May 1897 whereby the two powers agreed neither to disturb the *status quo* in the Balkans, nor to permit anyone else to do so; the Balkans were, for the next ten years, 'put on ice'. By 1900 Austria was firmly committed to the Triple Alliance, but as long as the Balkans remained quiet and Russia behaved cautiously, it was most unlikely that the connection with Germany would lead the Austrians to undertake an adventurous policy [220; 228].

No less surprising than the decision of Austria-Hungary to join Germany in the Dual Alliance of 1879 was the decision of Italy to join Austria-Hungary in the Triple Alliance of 1882. The Austrians had led the opposition to Italian unification throughout the nineteenth century: the Italian lands of Lombardy and Venetia were recaptured from the Austrians only by force of arms, and the Austrians had frequently intervened against the liberal and constitutional movements in the peninsula since 1815. A considerable change in outlook was necessary in order for the Italians to overlook the recent past.

Moreover, Italian unification had not been completed in the wars of 1859 or 1866; *Italia irredenta** ('unredeemed Italy') remained [258]. The Austrians continued to hold on to the Tyrol, Trieste and Fiume (see Map 2 on p. 137) – all areas densely populated by Italians. In the eyes of some, therefore, Austria was still Italy's principal enemy [117]. But others had grievances against France. In exchange for French assistance to Piedmont-Sardinia in the war of 1859 against Austria, the Piedmontese had ceded Nice and Savoy – each with sizeable Italian populations – to France [242]. Some nationalists believed that Italy would not be complete until these territories were recaptured. The French had also damaged themselves in Italian opinion by maintaining and defending the papal possessions in and around Rome; in 1867 they had actually fought off an attack led by Giuseppe Garibaldi, the great Italian patriot, and then sent him into exile [256]. Only when the French needed all available manpower in their war with Prussia in 1870 did they withdraw their troops from Rome, thereby permitting the

Italians to capture it. In northern Italy, therefore, there remained lingering grievances against both Austria-Hungary and France, although most nationalists felt that the grievances against France were rather minor by comparison.

Dreams of neo-Roman greatness in the Mediterranean divided Italy from France more than the hope of recapturing Nice and Savoy, more than the issue of French troops guarding the papacy. One of the symbols of the Italian *Risorgimento** ('resurgence') was the past greatness of Rome, which seemed to show what the Italian people could achieve if they were united with one another and free from foreign interference. Even the most fervent nationalists did not go so far as to suggest that it was possible to re-establish the Roman empire in Europe, but they did believe that Italy had a special mission to spread civilisation, and the Mediterranean territories of north Africa, where the Ottoman empire was steadily disintegrating, offered an attractive site for the demonstration of Italy's renewed greatness [253]. The strongest component of Italian imperialism was backward-looking: visions of a *mare nostrum*, of making the Mediterranean an Italian sea – as it had been in the glorious days of the Roman Empire – were always stronger than coldly rational calculations of financial and economic benefits [246].

Italy, following unification, was more concerned with questions of prestige and status than was any other great power. Indeed, the fundamental question facing Italy after 1866 was whether or not she was in fact a 'great' power. She had been united by war, but not by victories: defeats on the battlefield were compensated for by victories in diplomacy. Judged by any measurable criteria Italy was certainly the least of the Great Powers in 1900: she had the smallest army [248]; she was the least populous; her iron and steel production was not only the smallest, but amounted to only one-fifth of Austria-Hungary's, and one-tenth of Russia's [243]. Italy was still an agricultural nation, yet she did not produce enough food to feed herself; her railway system was undeveloped and inadequate; her ports had not been modernised; she could not supply her own energy needs [251]. It is difficult to believe that Italy could be regarded as a great power when Spain and Belgium were not, and yet Italian politicians were determined to achieve this status by behaving in the way that a great power was supposed to behave [249].

An empire in the Mediterranean would go far to establishing Italy's claim to great-power status, and this was the essential factor in drawing Italy into the combination with Austria-Hungary and

Germany [108]. Membership of the Triple Alliance by itself did much to support Italy's claim to this status, and the terms of the 1882 agreement were highly attractive to her. In return for promising to support Germany, were Germany to be attacked by France, Italy received a guarantee of German and Austrian support should France attack her. The only real concession that Italy made to her alliance partners was her promise to remain neutral if one of them came to be engaged in a war with a single power: in other words, she would not take advantage of a war between Austria-Hungary and Russia to attack the Austrians in the hope of redeeming Tyrol, Trieste and Fiume. In this first phase of the alliance, Italy's role was clearly defensive [*Doc. 2*].

But Italy, in spite of the practical limitations she faced, had great ambitions. The original version of the Triple Alliance, which did nothing to promise that any of these ambitions would be fulfilled, would have to be revised if Italy were to succeed with her dreams of expanding along the southern shores of the Mediterranean. Some hint of this was given in 1887 when the Triple Alliance was renewed and a new agreement was arranged between Italy and Austria-Hungary that promised 'reciprocal compensations' should the *status quo* of the Balkans be altered. This did something to satisfy Italian hopes of expanding along the shore of the Adriatic. More encouraging still was a new agreement with Germany that promised both military assistance to Italy, should she become embroiled in a war with France over Tunis or Morocco, and diplomatic assistance in securing for Italy improvements in her frontier security and maritime position: that is, the irredentist claims against France in Nice, Savoy and Corsica, and the Mediterranean ambitions in Tunis. After 1887 it appears that Italy stood to make substantial gains in the event of hostilities with France or a disturbance of the Balkan *status quo*. Italy was not, therefore, one of the states determined to uphold the current territorial and political arrangements in Europe [262].

Italy's ambitions were limited only by her lack of power and her vulnerable geographical position. In spite of the favourable diplomatic arrangements with Germany and Austria-Hungary, few Italians believed that they could afford to engage in a war in which Great Britain was an enemy [247]. Many of Italy's largest cities (Naples, Palermo, Genoa, Venice), were open to naval bombardment; much of her railway system (as underdeveloped as this was) hugged the coastline; she depended on maritime commerce to make up for her inability to feed herself and for the absence of coal supplies with which to fuel her industry. Italy had to be certain, therefore, that in a war with France she could count on Britain's assistance or at least her neutrality. This hope seemed to have been realised in the Mediterranean agreement of February 1887 which, although referring rather vaguely to consultation and co-operation, did draw Italy and Britain closer together. Italy, even more than Austria-Hungary and Germany, needed Britain to join the Triple Alliance.

The question facing Italy in 1900 was whether or not her continued membership in the Triple Alliance would enable her to fulfil some of her ambitious plans for expansion. As long as Britain remained even an informal friend of the alliance it seemed a useful instrument. But were Britain to switch sides, it would be a dangerous policy for Italy to run the risk of a war with both Britain and France. The other members of the Triple Alliance were keenly aware that Italy always had the alternative of joining France and Russia and focusing her ambitions on the Tyrol and the Adriatic rather than on the Mediterranean. Italy was apparently locked into the Triple Alliance; in reality she would be tempted to disengage if it appeared too dangerous or if a more attractive offer were made [243; 250].

3   THE DUAL ALLIANCE

The joining together of France and Russia in the Dual Alliance of 1894 was a revolutionary event in the history of European diplomacy, and one that fundamentally altered the pattern of relations. Few observers had believed such an alliance to be possible. Philosophically, France and Russia represented opposite ends of the political spectrum: France stood for revolution and republicanism, Russia for stability and despotism. Nor was this clash of ideas purely symbolic. Russian statesmen believed that all threats to the tsarist regime and to the stability of European politics emanated from Paris; French statesmen believed that their republican system and a morally legitimate European order would always be imperilled by the existence of the Russian autocracy*. Nor were these fears purely imaginary: France had invaded Russia twice during the nineteenth century, in 1812 and in 1854; Russia had led the anti-revolutionary movement, creating the Holy Alliance in 1815 and crushing the Hungarian revolution in 1848. When the two states committed themselves to assist one another if either were to be attacked, therefore, they implicitly announced the triumph of interests over ideas. In order to understand the origins of the First World War it is essential to understand what these interests were and how each of these two great powers believed their alliance would provide for their achievement.

Foreign observers of nineteenth-century Russia were invariably struck by two features of Russia as a great power. Those from western Europe, especially from Britain and France, were struck by the nature of the tsarist autocracy, which seemed to them to give a distinctive coloration to Russian foreign policy, designed as it was to uphold the legitimacy of the regime. They were also sensitive to the enormous power of Russia, although observers from central Europe, especially from Prussia and Austria, were more likely to be fascinated by this feature. Whether this power was real or imagined, and whether or not the autocratic nature of the Russian regime predetermined the direction of her policy were crucial questions for European diplomats in the late nineteenth century.

The part played by Russia in the destruction of the empire of Napoleon I contributed enormously to her reputation as a great power up to the time of the Crimean War. Although Napoleon had defeated each of the states of continental Europe and proven himself invulnerable to the continuing hostility of Great Britain, his *grande armée* had been annihilated when he had attempted to invade Russia. From the original invasion force of 600,000 only 100,000 had returned. Europeans as a whole drew two conclusions from this, the most destructive military episode in European history before the First World War: that the territorial expanse of Russia was so immense that a successful invasion was almost unimaginable; and that the population of Russia was so huge that she could suffer the most appalling losses and live to fight another day. Thus, although Napoleon penetrated as far as Moscow, and although he managed to capture the city, and although Russia lost 200,000 men in a single battle at Borodino, Russia was not defeated. Within three years of Napoleon launching his invasion of Russia, she had 30,000 of her troops participating in the allied occupation of France.

The advantages in population and territory that had enabled Russia to withstand the French invasion persisted, or grew, throughout the century. Her territory dwarfed that of continental Europe. Her population, in 1900, numbered twice as much as that of her nearest rival, Germany, and was almost equal to the combined population of Germany, Austria-Hungary and Italy. In 1900 the Russian empire comprised some 16 million square miles and contained approximately 125 million people.

The raw components of power seemed to suggest that Russia was capable of overwhelming any potential opponents on the European continent, and the Germans and Austrians were certainly sensitive to the dangerous proximity of the Russian giant. But power, in order to be effectively applied, depends on more than size alone, and here contemporaries in 1900 were much less certain about the actual strength of Russia. Modern armies and navies were in the process of becoming industrial machines. They required railways and coal to move them, iron and steel to arm and supply them, and, in these components of power, Russia was noticeably behind the other great powers. In 1910 European Russia had less than one-tenth the length of railway per square kilometre of Britain or Germany. In 1900 her coal production was one-half that of Austria-Hungary, one-tenth that of Germany; her pig-iron production amounted to 40 per cent of the German, 33 per cent of the British; steel production to 30 per cent of the British, 20 per cent of the German. Given Russia's limited industrial development, it was questionable whether she would be able to utilise her advantage in manpower, and it was clear that the most difficult operation for her to mount would be one that required her to go quickly on to the offensive [264].

Critics of the regime blamed Russia's weakness on her autocratic system of government. In the decade prior to the revolution of 1905 a wide range of opposition groups emerged, all of them demanding fundamental changes in the nature of the regime. Marxists established the Russian Social Democratic Labour Party in 1898, which aimed to overthrow the tsar by harnessing the revolutionary potential of the proletariat. Liberals published a newspaper, *Liberation*, beginning in 1902, and organised the Union of Liberation in 1904, which aimed to abolish the autocracy and establish constitutional government. Populists united several factions in 1901 when they organised the Party of Socialist Revolutionaries, dedicated to the triumph of the 'will of the people', which was to be achieved through the use of terror and by mobilising the peasant masses of the countryside [266].

As varied as these opposition groups were, and in spite of their differences with one another, they were nevertheless united in their belief that social justice was impossible under the tsarist autocracy. Moreover, they believed that Russia could never be transformed into a modern state as long as the tsar and his landowning aristocracy remained in control. Thus, the Russian people would continue to find themselves at the mercy of their better-organised and better-equipped neighbours, as they had during the invasions of 1812 and 1854 [263].

The tsar, by contrast, rested much of his right to govern on the claim that he and his ancestors were responsible for the creation of the Russian state, and that the autocracy, in alliance with the gentry, was essential to its maintenance and defence. This claim made the tsar and his advisers peculiarly sensitive to international questions. If the regime suffered a defeat in diplomacy, the reverberations might shake the autocracy to its foundations: disenchantment within Russia was most intense in the immediate aftermath of disastrous foreign adventures – following the Crimean War of 1855–56, the war with Turkey of 1877–78, and the war with Japan in 1905. The tsar was fully aware of the dangers that lurked within any policy of adventure, especially after 1905, but he was also aware that his other claim to authority, his leadership of the Christians of the Orthodox church, would suffer if he failed to act on behalf of his brethren when they were endangered by the Muslims of the Ottoman empire. Too cautious a policy might be as dangerous as one that was too adventurous [267].

These twin claims to authority – the traditional powers of the monarch and the leadership of the Orthodox church – were nicely fused together in the Holy Alliance created by Tsar Alexander I in 1815. The alliance, which was a highly informal arrangement, initially included Russia, Austria and Prussia, and was supposed to guarantee that Christian principles would provide the foundation for rule in these states, and that the monarchs would work together to maintain peace and justice. Monarchical solidarity was to take the place of revolutionary republicanism and nationalism, while the right to rule was to be based on Christianity rather than the Rights of Man or the General Will. In the years following the Congress of Vienna, Russia came to be regarded as the bastion of reaction, and the upheavals that did occur – in Spain, in Italy, and even in Germany – were far removed from her own frontiers. Never was the strength of tsarist rule so vividly demonstrated as in 1848, when, practically free from the revolutionary uprisings that swept across Europe, Tsar Nicholas I was able to dispatch 130,000 troops to assist the Habsburg emperor in crushing the Hungarian revolt [270].

The idea of the Holy Alliance was an attractive one to Russia, both because it upheld the principle of the Christian monarchy and because it offered protection against attack by her neighbours [147]. It also appeared to provide a barrier against revolutionary infection from western Europe or against another Napoleon. It should not be surprising to discover, therefore, that some Russians in the decades before 1914 longed for a return to the peace and security of the Holy Alliance, to a policy of co-operation with Germany and Austria.

In spite of the alliance, an underlying tension between Russia and Austria had emerged early in the century, as the growing aspirations of Balkan Christians to set themselves free from Turkish rule and form their own states began to distinguish the politics of south-eastern Europe [*Doc. 10*]. Where Austria, following Metternich's principles, preferred to suppress upheavals and crush revolutions of any kind, Russia usually chose to support the demands of the Christians. This policy led to a particularly acute difference of opinion over the question of Greek independence in 1827. The tsar's inherited role of protector of the Christians in the Ottoman empire also led to war with France and Britain in 1854, when Nicholas I came to believe that Napoleon III was attempting to replace him as spokesman for the Christians at Constantinople; if this new Napoleonic strategy were to succeed, it could result in the sultan becoming a puppet of France and Britain. But where this would seem to have reinforced Russia's determination to rely upon the Holy Alliance against the western powers, the Crimean War destroyed that arrangement as an attractive strategy for Russia. Austria refused to act as the friend of Russia – in spite of Russian intervention having saved her from dissolution six years earlier – and took advantage of Russia's predicament to exploit the situation to her own advantage. During the war, and at the peace conference, Austria demonstrated that the principle of monarchical solidarity no longer mattered to her, and that she was more concerned with restraining Russian ambitions in the Balkans and in the Black Sea [110; 147].

After the Treaty of Paris brought the Crimean War to a close in 1856, Russian foreign policy became more 'realistic'*, less concerned with principles such as monarchical solidarity and orthodox rights, and more concerned with the interests and the security of the Russian state. The Crimean War had shown that Russia was more vulnerable to attack than the precedent of the Napoleonic invasion had indicated; France and Britain had avoided the disasters of 1812 by attacking in the south through the Straits. The naval strength of the western allies had enabled them to control the lines of communication and supply, which were practically invulnerable to counter-attack from Russia, and almost impervious to the Russian winter. Thus, the treaty of 1856 had attempted to perpetuate Russia's exposed position by 'neutralising' the Black Sea, by disallowing both Russian and Turkish warships from operating there. Like most neutrality arrangements, this one gave France and Britain a distinct advantage.

The lessons of the Crimean War laid new foundations for Russian foreign policy. Austria now came to be regarded as unreliable or unfriendly, while Britain emerged as Russia's real competitor. The political course of the war led to the conclusion that the British, and not the Russians or the French, had achieved paramount influence at Constantinople. Moreover, Britain's strategy in the eastern Mediterranean made it appear that she was willing to use this influence to threaten Russia in the Black Sea whenever she found it useful to do so [154]. The new realism in Russian policy meant establishing a counterpoise to Britain in the Black Sea by undertaking a forward policy in central Asia in order to threaten the British empire in India [266; 341].

The new realism also meant working closely with Bismarck. Prussia had not joined the Crimean coalition and, especially after the Austro-Prussian War of 1866, she seemed to offer a useful counterpoise to Austria. A strong tradition of friendship with Prussians existed at the Russian court (where many nobles were married to Germans); Prussia seemed to have no ambitions in the Balkans or in the Black Sea, and the two states had a history of co-operation in subduing their Polish subjects whenever trouble broke out [207]. Russia's new realism was rewarded in 1870 when, in return for her remaining neutral during the Franco-Prussian War, Bismarck led the way in securing international agreement to the annulment of the Black Sea clauses. As long as Bismarck was prepared to keep a close rein on Austria in the Balkans and to act as the 'honest broker' in Austro-Russian arguments, the Russians were happy to co-operate with him – a state of affairs that was most clearly symbolised when Alexander II and Franz Joseph met with Wilhelm I in Berlin and declared their friendship in the *Dreikaiserbund* (Three Emperors' League) of 1871 [131; 132].

But the meeting of the three emperors did not renew the Holy Alliance. After the betrayal of 1854–56, Russia would never again trust Austria, and, insofar as Russian policy retained any ideological foundation, this moved away from monarchical solidarity and in the direction of panslavism. The second half of the nineteenth century witnessed the rise of the 'slavic idea' which saw Russia as a state culturally and politically distinct from the states of western and central Europe. Russia, according to this view, had an historic mission to protect and promote – perhaps even to unite – all Slav peoples, which meant defending the interests of Bulgars, Serbs and Montenegrins. This idea, which was a more extreme, modernised version of the older notion of an Orthodox brotherhood of believers, became increasingly popular among Russian educated classes, even though it inevitably meant antagonism with both the Ottoman and Habsburg empires. When Wilhelm II acceded to the throne in 1888 and quickly launched Germany on its new course in foreign policy, a large part of which involved the expansion of German interests in the Ottoman empire and more straightforward support of Austria-Hungary, the germanophiles in Russia found it increasingly difficult to maintain the connection with Germany in the face of slavophile* sentiments [269; 279].

The new course in German policy also reflected the changing nature of the balance of power in Europe, which further altered Russia's perception of the position she occupied in that balance.

Germany's decisive victory over France in 1870–71 showed that she was now the pre-eminent military state on the continent and, over the next twenty years, the gap between Germany and France continued to grow. Russia's professional diplomatists increasingly became convinced that Germany intended to harness this new strength, and, if Germany crushed France altogether, she would be free to pursue a much more aggressive policy in the east. This was particularly true given the signs that the Habsburg empire was being transformed into a German satellite, rather than an equal partner, and that Britain was co-operating with the Triple Alliance in the middle east and in the Mediterranean. A strong and independent France, even if she did follow the dangerous creed of republicanism, was seen by Russian diplomats as a necessary counterbalance to German power. Overcoming a century of tradition, therefore, Russia signed, on 4 January 1894, an alliance with France that provided for mutual defence against a German attack, or an Austrian attack (on Russia) that was supported by Germany, or an Italian attack (on France) that was supported by Germany [*Doc. 6*] [264].

The French found it as difficult to overcome their aversion to the tsarist autocracy as the Russians had found it to overcome their horror of revolutionary republicanism. Throughout the nineteenth century, no state had so clearly symbolised the decadence of the *ancien régime* as Russia. The Russian emperor claimed that his right to rule came from God, whereas both Napoleon I and Napoleon III claimed that their mandate came from the people. Russia was still stuck in the mire of unenlightened, theocratic* ideas: the Orthodox church was the most backward in Europe; no representative institutions existed whereby the people could make their will known; ordinary people were treated as chattels, not as citizens. The French came to believe that an implicit connection existed between the survival of the autocracy in Russia and the unregenerate nature of the whole European system. The failure of the principles of the French revolution could be traced to the strength of the tsarist regime; its disappearance could open the door to a new Europe.

In the nineteenth century, Paris became the home of Russian revolutionaries: anarchists*, nihilists* and communists organised secret societies, published newspapers, and plotted the overthrow of the tsar, none of which could have happened without the tacit support of the French government [*Doc. 5*] [278]. The cause of Polish nationalism in particular was close to many French hearts; the partition of Poland in the era before the French Revolution, carried out by the despots of the east against the wishes of the Polish people, symbolised the wickedness of the old regime. France became the champion of the cause of Polish independence and the home of the movement. When the people of Paris erupted in the final days of the Franco-Prussian War and formed a revolutionary commune, and when this was followed by the establishment of the Third French Republic, it seemed to confirm the impression that France would always be inflammable, chaotic and fanatical.

Bismarck certainly counted on this continuing to be the case. Assuming that the French would do anything to avenge the humiliating defeat they had suffered at the hands of the Prussians, he regarded Russian fears of revolution as one of the tools he could use to keep them away from the French. Moreover, the habitual instability of the French political system ought to provide insurance against a cohesive national campaign to recover their strength. Although the Franco-Russian alliance proved that differences in political ideology were not sufficient to overcome calculations based on strategic interest, the idea that France was in decline before the First World War, and that this was one of the fundamental factors that determined the international politics of the period, has become indelibly etched upon the history of Europe from 1871 to 1914.

Like most legends, that of French decline has much to support it. At the time of the Franco-Prussian War, the two states had been roughly equal in population, but by 1914 Germany was almost double the size of France, which was now only slightly larger than Italy, and somewhat smaller than Austria-Hungary. In both iron and steel production France and Germany were equals in 1870–71, but by 1914 France produced only 30 per cent as much iron and only 25 per cent as much steel. The balance that had appeared to exist when the Franco-Prussian War broke out had clearly disappeared by 1914. Contemporary observers concluded that France was no longer in a position to dominate Europe, and that her place as the dominant European power had been taken over by Germany [110].

But the weakness of France is easily exaggerated, and it is important to recognise that few Frenchmen believed their nation to be finished as a great power in the era before 1914. The French people in general, and republicans in particular, attributed the defeat of 1870–71 to the corruption and incompetence of Napoleon III and his advisers. According to this view, France and Prussia had been equals in 1870–71, so defeat on the battlefield was not predetermined by factors beyond anyone's control: on the contrary, the politicians of the Second Empire (and those they appointed to positions of military command) had been corrupted by their appetite for wealth and power. The leaders of the new republic denounced their predecessors as depraved seekers of pleasure and luxury; they sought instead to create a regime that would be moral, efficient and unified, a regime in which all Frenchmen could take pride and which, consequently, would benefit from a renewed patriotic fervour [315].

The first problem confronting the new republic was the payment of the huge indemnity provided for in the Treaty of Frankfurt; until this was paid a German army of occupation would remain in France. Bismarck had hoped that the indemnity would throw French finances into such disorder as to make their recovery long and hard. The French people, however, unlike the Germans after 1919, chose to regard payment as a matter of national honour and, against all expectations, paid the indemnity in a little over two years – six months ahead of schedule. Nor did this impoverish the nation. Over the next forty years the French showed that, in spite of their lagging industrial productivity, they enjoyed sufficient reserves of capital (as a result of the national preoccupation with saving rather than spending) to remain a leading participant in the European economy. Iron and steel do not account for everything, and the ability of the Paris *bourse* to float loans was an important factor in the events that led up to the Franco-Russian alliance [300].

French money also made it possible to expand and modernise the army with unexpected speed, and to an extent that frightened Bismarck. Within a year of the French defeat, the new republican Chamber of Deputies agreed that they could afford to introduce compulsory five-year military service for all men between the ages of twenty and forty. For the next thirty years France consistently spent more money on her army than Germany did, and at least twice as much on her navy. By 1900 France's regular army was slightly larger than Germany's. The tremendous growth of Germany's economy and population undoubtedly provided her with a potential greater than that of France – but this might count for little if she could be defeated quickly on the battlefield.

The French national recovery – at least as it was measured in troops and armaments – was achieved at a tremendous cost however, as French taxpayers regularly paid almost twice as much as their German counterparts. The cost of military parity no doubt contributed to the gap in the economic development of the two nations, which continued to grow each year. Nevertheless, French patriotic pride (combined with gold reserves) gave France a military standing almost equal to that of Germany in 1900 [284; 295].

The revival of patriotism after 1871 also stimulated colonial expansion. At the time of France's defeat, her overseas empire consisted of no more than a handful of ports and islands along the coasts of Africa and China; by 1900 the French had expanded their empire to the extent that it comprised four million square miles – an empire second only to that of Great Britain and more than twenty times the size of France itself. Vast territories were marked out in north Africa, west Africa and Indo-China, and a large navy was built to defend the new possessions. Until the late 1880s France was spending almost as much as Britain on her navy, and more than Germany, Austria-Hungary, Italy, Russia and the United States combined.

The new imperialism in France, the reformed and expanded army, the new and modern navy, the readiness to use accumulated capital for political purposes, along with pride in the political achievements of the Third Republic, contribute to a rather different picture of France from 1870 to 1900. Far from resembling a state whose citizens were conscious of its steady decline, France can be seen as spirited and determined, eager to overcome the reputation for weakness and corruption that she had acquired as a result of the débâcle of 1870 [294; 305].

The great revival following 1870 was neither simple nor straightforward. Colonial expansion encouraged quarrels with Britain, and one of these, the Fashoda crisis, almost led to war in 1898 (see below, p. 45). Meanwhile, those who sought *revanche* persisted in seeing Germany as the real enemy, which led the Germans to anticipate that any conflict in Europe would encourage the French to attack them [307]. Those who looked overseas for the future of France as a great power usually saw Britain as the enemy, and therefore supported the building of a large fleet; the same reasoning also ought to have led them to support a *rapprochement** with Germany in Europe. Those who believed that French power and dignity could be restored only by recapturing the lost provinces of Alsace and Lorraine clearly regarded Germany as the enemy, and therefore supported the creation of a large army; the same reasoning also ought to have led them to support the settlement of colonial differences with Britain overseas [291; 296].

From 1870 to 1900, however, the French attempted to pursue continentalism and colonialism simultaneously. There was no clear or consistent leadership to provide a systematic approach to foreign affairs. Although the republic itself proved to be stable, successfully withstanding challenges from monarchists and Bonapartists alike, the governments of the republic were much less so: they lasted for little more than a year at a time in the first two decades after 1871. France had thirteen foreign ministers in the nineteen years between 1871 and 1890. This political instability resulted in a confused policy that managed to antagonise both Germany and Britain, which, in turn, contributed significantly to the Anglo-German harmony that prevailed throughout most of this period.

Anglo-French relations, which had improved dramatically after 1871, were seriously damaged when the British occupied Egypt in 1882. A financial crisis had caused the bankruptcy of the Egyptian government in 1876, whereupon France and Britain had agreed to participate in joint financial control. But this broke down in 1882 when a nationalist revolt seemed to threaten the security of the Suez Canal, leading the British to intervene by force. However, the French, who had agreed to act jointly with Britain, were prevented from participating when the government lost a vote in the Chamber of Deputies. Although the deputies were not prepared to undertake the expense of a joint occupation, there was widespread resentment at the establishment of British predominance in Egypt. Ever since Napoleon's invasion of 1798 the French had come to regard themselves as having a special mission to perform in Egypt. One of the glories of Napoleon III's Second Empire had been the building of the Suez Canal, and French investment in Egypt had continued to grow since 1871. Even if the deputies were not keen on a new French intervention in Egypt, the permanent officials of the Quai d'Orsay* (the French foreign ministry), who really managed policy in the absence of strong governments, were mostly keen colonialists. Many officials believed that the way to restore the greatness of France was to establish a great empire in north Africa that would stretch from Morocco to Egypt, thus transforming her into the greatest power in the Mediterranean. For twenty years following the British intervention, therefore, the foreign ministry was preoccupied with prying the British out of Egypt [288].

The Germans, not surprisingly, welcomed the Anglo-French antagonism over Egypt, and Bismarck encouraged the French to enlarge their interests in Tunisia, Morocco, Nigeria, Madagascar and Indo-China. Consequently, the years immediately after 1882 were ones of Franco-German *détente*. But French policy was inconsistent: *revanche* was not dead. Although a growing number of responsible French politicians were inclined to forget the lost provinces, few dared to proclaim this publicly; the cause of Alsace and Lorraine still fired the imaginations of too many Frenchmen for this to be a practicable programme, a point which was illustrated in the 'Boulanger affair' of 1889.

General Boulanger was an outspoken nationalist who, as minister of war in 1886–87, initiated further reforms and expansion of the army. He became an immensely popular figure, especially with those extreme patriots who believed that France had already recovered sufficiently to launch a war of revenge on Germany [274]. Bismarck was particularly worried by his popularity, because it seemed to presage the kind of Bonapartist revival that might prove a real threat – a strong man who could unite the country in an anti-German crusade. Although Boulanger lost his nerve and abandoned the idea of a *coup d'état* against the republic, his momentary fame led to an expansion of the German army, and to talk of a preventive war against France [289; 290].

The Boulanger affair made it clear to the Germans that any *détente* with France was likely to be short-lived; in spite of their colonial aspirations, the French, it seemed, would never be persuaded to think of Germany as anything but an enemy. By the 1890s few Frenchmen were prepared to undertake an aggressive campaign to restore the lost provinces – but neither were they prepared to abandon them permanently to Germany. The war-scare that arose from the Boulanger affair led the French to fear that the Germans would attempt to confirm their possession of Alsace-Lorraine by launching a new war against them [290].

In spite of the revival of French spirits, finances and military forces following 1871, France remained as isolated diplomatically as she had been during the war itself. Where Bismarck had succeeded in building the Triple Alliance and bringing Russia and Britain into association with it via the *Dreikaiserbund* and the Mediterranean agreements, the French had managed only to antagonise Britain and Italy. In the first instance, the great attraction of an alliance with Russia was that it would not force the French to choose between their colonial ambitions and their hopes of recovering the lost provinces: the Russians had been consistently anti-English since 1856, and, with the abandonment of the Russo-German Reinsurance Treaty in 1891, the Russians were prepared to consider French suggestions for a defensive alliance against Germany. The alliance really did nothing to provide for *revanche*, but it did offer security against another German attack. Security in Europe encouraged the French to become more aggressive overseas, and within a few years they found themselves on the brink of war with Britain.

The French colonialists believed, after almost twenty years of fruitless diplomatic efforts to persuade the British to leave Egypt, that they must find some way to prod them into serious negotiations. The strategy they resolved upon was to send a military expedition through the Congo into the Sudan. Here they could, by occupying a position at the headwaters of the Nile, threaten the British position in Egypt. They believed that only a threat would be necessary – but they were mistaken. When the French force arrived at Fashoda (see Map 4 on p. 139) in September 1898 it was challenged by a superior British force, and the British government instantly made clear its determination to go to war rather than permit the French to remain in the Sudan. The French, who were not prepared for war with the British in Africa or on the high seas, had no choice but to back down and retreat from the Sudan [308].

By 1900, therefore, French policy was still somewhat uncertain, although almost everyone who mattered now regarded it as essential that the alliance with Russia be maintained. The colonial party used the example of Fashoda to encourage a *rapprochement* with Germany and to argue that the alliance with Russia ought to be expanded to include the contingency of war with Britain. The Franco-Russian alliance was, accordingly, altered in this way in 1899 [119]. The object of the alliance was also expanded to provide for the maintenance of 'the balance of power in Europe' in the hope of forestalling direct German control of the Habsburg monarchy. Whether the French ought to concentrate their attention on the German threat to their security in Europe or on the British competition to their ambitions in Africa had not yet been resolved. Temporarily, the French hoped that their alliance with Russia would prove strong enough to permit them to pursue both objects simultaneously.

4 GREAT BRITAIN

By 1900, continental Europe had been clearly divided into two rival alliances, but one great power had refused to join either side. Instead, Britain was at that moment engaged in fighting a war in South Africa – a fact that led some critics of the government to deplore the 'isolation' that left her not only without allies, but practically without friends. Critics worried that this isolation would render Britain vulnerable, that the animosity felt for the British cause in the Anglo-Boer War might lead to the formation of a 'continental league' aimed at the British empire, and perhaps to a new version of Napoleon's continental system. After all, they pointed out, France and Russia, Germany and Italy, all coveted territories contained within the empire. Nor was isolation necessary: Germany, Austria-Hungary and Italy had been attempting to persuade Britain to join the Triple Alliance for a decade or more. Britain, however, had steadfastly refused to join, and leading members of the government were, by the time of the Anglo-Boer War, proclaiming that her isolation was 'splendid' [324].

Was it a sign of British strength or weakness that she was isolated in 1900? Continental observers of Britain in the late nineteenth century were particularly struck by three aspects of Great Britain as a great power: her industry, her empire, and her navy. These components were understood to work in close conjunction with one another: Britain's industry provided the appetite for empire, the desire for the resources and markets that her possessions in Africa and Asia, in North America, the Caribbean and Australasia provided; industrial prosperity and technological proficiency enabled the British to construct a large, modern navy; mastery of the seas enabled them to defend their empire against all opponents. This simplistic picture may be misleading, but the idea that British power was fundamentally industrial, and that British interests were essentially imperial, was entertained by most observers of Victorian Britain [356]. What was debatable at the turn of the century was whether or not her power was sufficient to enable Britain to continue to stand aloof from the system of European alliances and alignments.

British industry was still pre-eminent in the Europe of 1900. Britain produced more coal than the five powers of the continent combined. She produced as much iron as the Triple Alliance, and only Germany produced more steel. In spite of the advantage she still enjoyed, however, the continental states in general, and Germany in particular, were rapidly closing the gap. In 1870 Britain had produced five times as much coal as all of Europe, and twice as much iron; in 1880 she had produced twice as much steel. Although British production in all of these vital sectors of the economy rose steadily in the fifty years prior to 1914, by the time war broke out Germany was producing almost as much coal, more iron and twice as much steel. In the newer, more technically oriented chemical and electrical industries Britain was outdistanced from the start, and was falling farther behind each year.

This changing pattern of industrialisation has led some commentators to argue that the First World War was simply an Anglo-German contest for industrial predominance and the trade that followed from it. But Russia too was making rapid strides in catching up with Britain and, outside Europe, the United States had already surpassed Britain in all of the vital industrial components by 1900. In spite of the continuing prosperity of British industry in 1900, therefore, it cannot be argued that it any longer provided Britain with a clear advantage over potential rivals.

The British empire, on the other hand, appeared in a quite different light. Without the empire Great Britain was a state not much bigger, either in territory or in population, than Italy; with the empire she was bigger than Russia. The enormous extent of the empire – over ten million square miles – gave Britain potential reserves of manpower and resources not available to the continental states, and most particularly not to the Central Powers. Colonial groups in Germany, France and Italy argued that they too must acquire empire in order to compete with Britain.

But the apparent advantages of empire might also be misleading, and possession of these vast territories could be interpreted as a source of weakness. They were certainly a source of danger: Russia, and the United States could threaten various parts of the empire much more easily than Britain could defend them; France apparently aimed to make trouble everywhere she could, especially in Egypt and Indo-China. Britain, who had fought wars against each of these states in the course of the nineteenth century, was forced to take τ.., ,nsive measures to defend her possessions against these threats. And now, near the end of the nineteenth century, new competitors emerged on the scene: Germany, Japan and Italy had also developed an appetite for empire, and they were now in a position to cause trouble and even greater expense to Britain, should they choose to do so. The British, in order to prepare to meet any or all of these threats (whether real or imagined) were compelled to erect fortifications and maintain defences in the far east, in central Asia, in Egypt, in the Mediterranean, in South Africa, on the Pacific coast of North America and elsewhere.

Critics of empire within Britain, of whom J.A. Hobson was the most famous, argued that the expense of such undertakings was out of all proportion to the benefits gained, that empire was a source of weakness, not strength. The greatest expense arose from the necessity of building a large navy to defend imperial possessions, and Hobson argued that naval interests – the Admiralty, ship-builders and port towns – were among the select groups that actually benefited from empire; everyone (especially the working classes) paid the taxes that were necessary to sustain the empire, but only special interests reaped the rewards. Radicals also argued that a large navy was not really essential for the defence of the British Isles, that a small navy and defensive fortifications were sufficient to deter an invasion; so Britain would be safer and more prosperous without the empire.

As the existence of the empire meant preparing for an imperial war, it was not enough that the British be superior to only one European competitor: the Royal Navy must be stronger than any possible combination of European navies. In the 1890s this meant building to the 'Two-Power Standard' in order to meet the threat of a combined Franco-Russian attack. But, after the German naval laws of 1898 and 1904, Germany too had to be taken into account, and the new dreadnought* class of battleship meant a further increase in the already enormous expenditure. By 1910 Great Britain was spending almost as much on her navy as Germany, France and Russia combined, and more than all six European great powers had spent in 1890 [327].

Naval building and imperialism had become controversial subjects in Britain by 1900, and the debate over the Anglo-Boer War had divided the Liberal party into distinct factions. Public controversy over the course of foreign policy was not a new feature of British political life, however, and foreign observers had noted throughout the nineteenth century the extent to which the British parliamentary system encouraged division and debate. The government was required to inform, explain and defend its foreign policy to members of parliament, but whether this was a source of strength or weakness in the making of policy, or a factor encouraging isolation rather than commitment, is very difficult to judge. Most members of parliament believed that they must conduct themselves cautiously and responsibly when it came to questions of foreign policy, that the foreign secretary and his advisers had access to better sources of information than they, and that the public would disapprove if criticism weakened the government's ability to negotiate successfully.

Ironically then, while there was more open discussion and criticism of foreign policy in Britain than anywhere in Europe (with the possible exception of France), there was also more continuity and coherence. Changes in government seldom meant dramatic changes in policy, and the party in power could usually be quite certain that the nation as a whole would support its policies. This coherence was largely the result of the widespread acceptance within the British ruling class of certain basic assumptions that were to guide British relations with Europe. Such debates as there were usually focused on methods, on questions of administration and organisation; the principles of the balance of power, of a strong navy, and of avoiding commitments that would draw Britain into a European war were generally supported by both political parties and most politicians. A century of unparalleled power and prosperity had furnished convincing evidence that adherence to these principles had accounted for Britain's success; it would be reckless to abandon them now.

The Napoleonic Wars had clarified the dangers with which Britain would be faced should one state succeed in establishing hegemony in Europe. Britain's economy had been severely disrupted by the interruption of trade with her best markets, which, in spite of the empire, were always to be found in Europe, and through the necessity of spending enormous sums on defence. Furthermore, there was little question that, had Napoleon succeeded in establishing real dominance and bending the whole of the European economy to suit the needs of France, he would eventually have been able to mount an effective challenge to Britain's overseas possessions, especially in India. No responsible Englishman believed that Britain could survive as a great power if Europe came under the control of France. Finally, economic hardship combined with inflammatory political ideas to produce the greatest danger of social revolution in Britain since the seventeenth century.

Security, prosperity and social harmony all seemed to depend upon what the British referred to as 'the balance of power'. This was a concept that was rooted in the eighteenth-century Enlightenment, and especially in the Newtonian concept of the physical universe. Ideally, the balance of forces among both heavenly bodies and states would regulate itself, but in the heavens divine intervention was sometimes necessary, as was occasional British intervention in European politics. The experience of the Napoleonic Wars furnished another lesson here: for intervention to be successful Britain needed to find one or more European allies – on her own she would not be able to defeat a continental power that possessed a great army. For the balance of power to work, therefore, Britain had to assume that one or more European states would always find it in their interest to counterbalance the power of the strongest; ideally, they would choose to do this on their own; if necessary, Britain would have to encourage them to do so.

In the forty years that followed the Congress of Vienna in 1815, the British demonstrated their belief in the principle of the balance of power. The French, once they accepted their 'historical' frontiers and gave up their ambitions to dominate Europe, became, in British eyes, respectable participants in the European system once again. The danger to the balance was now thought to come from Russia, which seemed to be in a position to dominate both eastern Europe, as her intervention in Hungary in 1848 demonstrated, and the middle east, as her policy in the crisis leading up to the Crimean War in 1854 seemed to show. Russia was transformed into an enemy, France into an ally.

The Crimean War has become almost synonymous with 'incompetence', and thus it is easy to forget that it was the only successful invasion of Russia in modern times. Britain achieved her basic aims: the Ottoman empire remained independent and relied more heavily on the advice of Britain than Russia; and the Habsburg empire was saved from declining to the level of a Russian satellite. The balance of power in Europe was maintained, but at the price of deeply rooted Russian animosity. For the next half-century everyone expected a great Anglo-Russian war, particularly as the Russians undertook to counter the neutralisation of the Black Sea that had been forced on them in 1856 by the Treaty of Paris by posing a counter-threat to the British empire in India. British foreign and defence policies for the next thirty years were devoted primarily to forestalling this Russian threat [343; 361].

Because the British had been concerned for more than a century with the threats posed by the French and the Russians, they were inclined to welcome the rise of Prussia and even the creation of the German empire. A strong Germany seemed to be just what Britain needed: situated as it was between France and Russia, it was perfectly suited to act as the fulcrum in the European balance of power. Moreover, unlike France and Russia, Germany had neither overseas interests nor a navy and therefore was unlikely to challenge either Britain's empire or her maritime supremacy. As long as Bismarck was satisfied with the post-1871 *status quo* in Europe, Germany was regarded as a 'natural' ally. The only undercurrent of concern emerged as a result of Germany's stunning victory over France in 1871: for Germany to be somewhat stronger than France suited British designs, but for the Germans to be able to overpower the French so quickly might cause complications. The British began to worry that German power might be so great as to render France subordinate in the future: another Franco-German war could even bring about the end of France as an independent state. This thinking led London to warn Berlin during the 'Is War in Sight?' crisis of 1875 that Britain would not remain indifferent if such a war were to take place [130; 142].

But after 1875 these worries began to recede as growing Anglo-Russian antagonism and the revival of French imperialism combined in such a way as to draw Britain closer to Germany and the Triple Alliance. In the 1880s and the 1890s, a possible German bid for hegemony in Europe seemed a much more unlikely threat than a Franco-Russian assault on the British empire. The Great Eastern Crisis of 1878 and the Penjdeh Crisis of 1886 convinced the British that the Russians still aimed to dominate the middle east and to place themselves in a position to threaten an invasion of India. Britain's occupation of Egypt in 1881 struck a blow to French pride and led to a series of bitter quarrels in Asia and Africa. As long as France and Russia faced the combined strength of the Triple Alliance in Europe, however, they were not likely to risk a conflict with Britain. In this way the balance of power contributed significantly to the defence of the British empire. And, as Russia and France appeared to be the restless, aggressive powers, determined to expand beyond Europe and to alter the balance within it, the British contributed to the stability of the Triple Alliance by assuring Italy and Austria-Hungary of their co-operation in the Mediterranean agreements of 1887 [325].

This state of affairs became less straightforward when Wilhelm II initiated his 'new course' in foreign policy [68]. Now Germany also appeared to have an interest in overseas expansion, and a series of minor Anglo-German disputes arose over places like Samoa, Togoland and the Cameroons. The British government never took these disputes very seriously, but the kaiser's highly publicised support for the Boers in South Africa, along with the German government's decision in 1898 to build a fleet, began to stimulate some opposition in Britain to the policy of co-operation with Germany. Throughout the 1890s, Germany had attempted to draw Britain into becoming a member of the Triple Alliance – a policy which seemed close to fruition with the Mediterranean agreements – but Britain had consistently refused to go any farther [328]. German entreaties had always been rejected, not because of germanophobia or the German bid for colonies, but because the British feared being drawn into a war in Europe for the sake of Germany's position in Alsace-Lorraine or Poland. Thus, when the war broke out in South Africa, the Germans began to promote the idea of a 'continental league' aimed at the British empire [322].

By 1900, therefore, the British found themselves isolated. Their traditional enemies, France and Russia, were allied with one another and had recently altered the terms of the alliance to provide for mutual action against the British. Their 'natural' ally, Germany, was increasingly antagonistic and apparently determined to cause them trouble wherever and whenever possible. The Anglo-Boer War demonstrated that this isolation posed little danger to the empire. The continental league amounted to nothing, and no joint action of the European powers was carried out; in fact, no action of any kind was taken against the British, who were able to fight the war in South Africa without worrying about the consequences in the far east, central Asia and the Mediterranean. The empire was never in any serious danger after 1900; Fashoda proved to be the last crisis in which Britain contemplated the possibility of a war with a European power arising from her imperial interests. The revolution in British diplomacy that took place after 1900 was sparked not by any immediate fear of a threat to the empire, but by concern for the European balance of power [329; 331].

PART THREE: THE EUROPEAN CRISIS

5   THE DIPLOMATIC REVOLUTION

The condition of European international relations was unusually simple and stable by 1900. The continent was clearly divided into two rival alliances: Germany, Austria-Hungary and Italy in the Triple Alliance; France and Russia in the Dual Alliance. Of the great powers, only Britain was unaccounted for. Everyone who engaged in diplomatic and military affairs regarded the alliance system as the primary characteristic of international relations, and every question that arose between 1900 and 1914 was assessed for its possible influence upon this system. After war broke out in 1914 many critics argued that the rival alliances made war inevitable, that sooner or later a crisis was certain to arise that would lead to a general European conflict, that it became increasingly difficult to minimise any friction or localise any controversy that arose in these years. The July crisis seemed the perfect illustration of this argument: what conceivable interest did Germany, Britain and France have in the fate of the Bosnian Serbs, other than the impact of the assassination on the alliance system?

But other observers saw the alliances as providing stability and predictability to the European system. Moreover, as the alliances were fundamentally defensive in nature, they reduced the likelihood of aggressive behaviour. The alliances also appeared to bolster the principle of the balance of power, which many still believed to be the best guarantee of peace: as long as neither side enjoyed a clear superiority over the other, they argued, no statesman would risk the destruction of modern war and possible social upheaval. This was an unpopular point of view after 1919, but the experience of the Cold War after 1945, when most of the world seemed divided into the rival alliances of NATO and the Warsaw Pact, in which localised conflicts became the norm, has given this perspective renewed strength.

Neither argument – that the alliances made war inevitable, or that they made the chances of it remote – can be tested. And the experience of the decade before the First World War demonstrates that simplistic assumptions about their impact are almost certainly false. To understand the alliance system, it must be located carefully within the context of the times.

The apparent stability of the system is deceptive. We know now that it endured, and that the pattern of the Central European Powers opposed by France and Russia that emerged in the 1890s was fundamentally the same as the conflict that broke out in 1914. Yet there were some significant changes. Italy, a member of the Triple Alliance for more than thirty years, went to war in 1915 against her former allies; Britain, independent of the alliance system in 1900 (and, if anything, enjoying better relations with Germany and Austria-Hungary than she did with France and Russia) joined the Dual Alliance against the Triple in 1914.

There were also noticeable differences within the alliances themselves, differences that led many to doubt whether they would remain intact. French interests and ambitions in north Africa were never approved by Russia, which was unlikely to support France in a war against Italy, Britain or Germany that began over Tunis, Egypt or Morocco; it was equally doubtful whether France would fight to support Russia in Manchuria or Korea. The Triple Alliance sometimes appeared to be coming apart at the seams: Italy could always be tempted to turn against Austria-Hungary if France offered her concessions; Austria-Hungary had no interest in supporting Germany's *Weltpolitik** ('world policy') in central and southern Africa, in China and the Pacific; some Germans argued that it was a mistake to support Austria-Hungary in the Balkans, that it was preferable to restore good relations with Russia and thereby disrupt the Franco-Russian alliance.

The alliance system appears in retrospect to have been more stable than it actually was. Significant changes took place between 1900 and 1914; diplomats frequently questioned the usefulness of the arrangements; each side worked to dismantle the foundations upon which the rival alliance had been built. Nevertheless, the broad outlines of the system remained intact because the basic pre-occupations of the great powers – their ambitions and their fears – survived the criticisms and the crises of the period from 1900 to 1914. It is as important to understand how the alliances withstood these challenges as it is to comprehend the differences that divided the partners.

As the Triple Alliance and the Dual Alliance alike had been constructed entirely for European reasons, it should come as no surprise that complications beyond the frontiers of western and eastern Europe made it difficult for them to operate cohesively. This was certainly true in the far east, where, in the summer of 1900, troubles that had been simmering in China for two years broke out in open rebellion. The 'League of Righteous and Harmonious Fists' (commonly referred to in the west as the 'Boxers'*), with the tacit support of China's dowager empress, murdered Christian missionaries in an anti-European campaign, marched on Peking and besieged the foreign legations there. On 21 June 1900, the Chinese government declared war on the foreign powers, and it looked for a moment as if a great war would be waged in China that might result in her dismemberment.

Germany in particular feared the possible consequences of the Boxer rebellion. Wilhelm II had committed himself to an active role in the far east in 1897 when, declaring that Germany was now a 'world power', he had seized the port of Tsingtao in Shantung province (see Map 3 on p. 138) [203]. If the rising led to the partitioning of China among the European powers, Germany's ambitious designs for the future were likely to be thwarted, as Russia, Britain and Japan had much stronger forces in the area. The Germans therefore proposed to the British that they should uphold the principle of the 'open door'* in China and maintain the integrity of the Chinese empire. The British, who did not wish to transform their sphere of influence in the Yangtse Valley into a protectorate unless they had no other choice, agreed, hoping that co-operation with Germany would prevent the Russians from seizing Manchuria, which they had occupied during the Boxer crisis. The Anglo-German agreement on China was duly signed on 16 October 1900.

British hopes of using Germany's friendship to forestall Russian expansion in China soon vanished. When the Russians refused to evacuate Manchuria, the German chancellor, Bernhard von Bülow, announced that the agreement with Britain was not intended to apply to Manchuria. What this really meant was that the Germans were not prepared to risk a crisis with Russia in Europe for the sake of their ambitions in the far east [194]. The British, who were currently embroiled in a colonial war with the Afrikaners (Dutch settlers) of South Africa, had already committed the bulk of their naval power and were in no position to forestall Russia on their own. They showed some interest, therefore, when, in March 1901, the Japanese approached them with the suggestion that they would be prepared to oppose the Russians in Manchuria if the British, in exchange, could keep the French neutral. The Japanese, who were determined to have Korea for themselves, believed that they could defeat the Russians if they did not have to face the combined fleets of Russia and France when attempting to land troops on the Chinese mainland.

An alliance with Japan offered some advantages to Britain, but these were not so obvious as they later appeared to be [363]. The British, in 1901, did not believe that Japan was strong enough to defeat Russia, even if France were neutralised. In November and December of 1901, therefore, the British foreign secretary, Lord Lansdowne, revived the idea of an alliance with Germany, but the Germans demanded too high a price: Britain must join the Triple Alliance [348]. The Germans were not going to run risks for the sake of the British empire without receiving some guarantees of support in Europe in exchange. Simultaneously, the Japanese were negotiating with the Russians on the basis of 'Man-Kan Kokan' – Japan to take Korea, Russia to take Manchuria [98]. These negotiations created a new scare for the British: a Russo-Japanese partition of China. Therefore, because the British could not prevent Russian expansion on their own, because German assistance depended on the British committing themselves to fighting France and Russia in Europe, and because a Russo-Japanese partition of China was the least desirable outcome of the crisis in the far east, the British chose to sign, on 30 January 1902, an alliance with Japan [*Doc. 9*].

The Anglo-Japanese alliance did not make war more likely: the Japanese believed that it would strengthen their bargaining position by making it clear to Russia that she would be forced to fight without an ally, should it come to war. But the men making the decisions in Russia were not in a cautious mood. Military adventurers, admirals and some speculators, arguing that Russia's future lay in far-eastern expansion, caught the ear of the tsar and stiffened his resolve not to compromise. Racism played a part in this decision, as the Japanese were thought to be racially inferior to the Europeans, and their surprising victory over the Chinese in 1895 was discounted accordingly. Moderates like the foreign minister, Count Lambsdorff, and the finance minister, Count Witte, were neglected in favour of the 'Korean' extremists, Bezobrazov, who was made a secretary of state, and Admiral Alexeiev, who was made viceroy of the far east.

Russia responded to the Anglo-Japanese alliance by signing a new version of her alliance with France. On 20 March 1902, a joint declaration was issued announcing, in effect, that the two would co-operate if a third party (Japan) threatened their interests by endangering the integrity of China. It was apparent to everyone that Russia was not going to back down without a fight. It also seemed apparent that the Franco-Russian alliance was in the process of being transformed from a limited arrangement, which was designed to meet the German challenge in Europe, into something more ambitious: an imperial design to establish Franco-Russian co-operation in Asia and, perhaps, in Africa.

The prospect of being drawn into a war against Britain for the sake of Russian interests in Manchuria and Korea was not a pleasant one for the French to contemplate [124]. Their view of the alliance with Russia had originally been 'European' but, ironically, after the Fashoda crisis demonstrated the failure of the alliance to operate outside Europe – Russia refusing any support against Britain – the French had proposed an expansion of its terms, and these had been incorporated into the alliance in 1899. The new terms, which provided for the possibility of a war with Britain, were in fact designed to avoid one. The French foreign minister, Delcassé, wished to expand the alliance in order to encourage the British to negotiate over Egypt and Morocco; its terms were not intended to draw France into a war.

Nevertheless, Delcassé had no choice but to agree when the Russians insisted that they issue the joint declaration of March 1902 [149]. France needed the alliance with Russia in order to avoid being reduced to the level of a German subordinate in Europe; nor would there be any hope of coercing the British into an agreement on north Africa without the prospect of Franco-Russian co-operation. While French foreign policy was guided skilfully by Delcassé from 1898 to 1905, it was coherent and consistent – in stark contrast with the period between 1871 and 1890, when thirteen different foreign ministers had presided over policy. Delcassé believed that French power and prestige could be re-established only by creating the great north-African empire envisioned by the Comité de l'Afrique Française*, and he at first attempted to achieve this by seeking the assistance of Germany, then by expanding the terms of the alliance with Russia [306]. But while he was conducting these diplomatic manoeuvres, Delcassé was aware of another option: perhaps the British would agree to settle their differences with France in Africa without the threat of war [285].

Delcassé's awareness of these options proved to be significant when, in the midst of the Russo-Japanese crisis in the far east, Morocco suddenly appeared ready to disintegrate. Tribes hostile to the sultan of Morocco revolted against his authority in late 1902 and he seemed powerless to stop them. Britain and France were equally fearful of the possible consequences of an uncontrolled revolt: Britain because it might threaten Gibraltar, France because it might threaten Algeria. Ironically, both turned to Germany for diplomatic support. But the Germans, who believed that Anglo-French quarrels would always work to their advantage, turned them both down. Hoping to exploit the Moroccan crisis, the Germans unwittingly encouraged an Anglo-French entente.

The first visible sign of an improvement in Anglo-French relations was the visit of King Edward VII to Paris in May 1903, which was a tremendous popular success. This was reciprocated when President Loubet and Delcassé travelled to London in July. The negotiations for a settlement of colonial differences, which began in earnest in the summer of 1903, were thus conducted in an atmosphere of public support. The displays of goodwill in both countries, while they were not responsible for the settlement that eventually emerged, certainly made the endeavours of the diplomats easier than had been expected [108].

The French would have found it more difficult to pursue a settlement with the British if the Russians had objected to the negotiations, but they did not. In part, Russia's attitude was the result of misplaced confidence in her strength in the far east: the 'Koreans' in the Russian government argued that they could defeat the Japanese without French assistance, as long as the British did not intervene. This argument was strengthened when the trans-Siberian railway was completed in August 1903, which made it seem that Russia would, for the first time, be able to transport troops and supplies quickly and efficiently to the far east.

But Russian strategy was not entirely 'Asiatic' or expansionist. The tsar and his military advisers had recently concluded that the existence of France as a great power was now vital to Russian security in Europe. In March 1901 Russian strategists predicted that France could not survive a war with Germany unless Russia mobilised rapidly and attacked Germany in the east. This thinking led to a new Russian mobilisation scheme, which was formally approved in November 1902. The Russian commitment to France remained firm. The Dual Alliance, which both parties had unsuccessfully attempted to utilise for purposes outside Europe – Russia in the far east, France in north Africa – nevertheless remained the most essential element in the European policy of each power.

Thus, when Japan attacked Russia at Port Arthur on 8 February 1904, it had little immediate impact upon power politics in Europe. Neither the Dual Alliance nor the Anglo-French colonial discussions were disrupted [113]. If anything, the Japanese attack only encouraged France and Britain to reach an agreement. In spite of Japan's initial victory at Port Arthur, no one was predicting that the Japanese could win the war – even though they enjoyed a naval superiority and their army outnumbered the Russian army of the far east by 330,000 to 100,000.

The discussions between Britain and France not only continued but were actually accelerated. The agreement, which was signed on 8 April 1904, resolved a wide range of Anglo-French differences in Newfoundland, Gambia, Nigeria, Madagascar, Siam and the New Hebrides [329]. But the essence of the agreement lay in the provisions pertaining to Egypt and Morocco. What the British wanted in Egypt was an end to the troublesome opposition of the French, both on Egypt's frontiers and within the committee of bondholders that was responsible for Egypt's financial affairs. Such a promise from France would reduce the expense involved in safeguarding Egypt and make it possible to continue with financial reform more quickly and more easily. In return, the French wanted the British to acknowledge their primacy in Morocco. In a secret protocol to the agreement, Britain promised that, should the sultan's authority in Morocco disappear, she would give France a free hand there, providing that the coastline opposite Gibraltar went to Spain and that this strip of territory would remain unfortified. The French, in other words, finally recognised the permanence of the British occupation of Egypt in exchange for the opportunity to establish their own occupation of Morocco.

The Anglo-French 'entente' was not an alliance. No enemy was singled out. No contingencies were provided for. No co-ordinated activities were planned. The entente was simply a settlement of colonial disputes that had been simmering for the last quarter-century. Such a scheme had surfaced repeatedly during these years, but had never emerged successfully because of French intransigence on the Egyptian question. France, in fact, conceded little in Egypt: the British occupation had become stable and, under the guiding hand of Lord Cromer, progressive [335]. What the French gave up was a dream, and this was the true significance of the entente. Anglo-French antagonism had been one of the steady factors upon which European diplomats and strategists had come to rely. The end of the antagonism was bound to cause reverberations throughout the international system. But in 1904 no one imagined that this would end with millions of British troops fighting alongside their French allies in a continental European war [293].

The Anglo-French entente did not signify a diplomatic revolution; it did no more than suggest that one might be possible. But there were other signs of important changes going on at the same time. In the midst of the Anglo-French negotiations, Russian and Austro-Hungarian representatives met at Murzsteg in October 1903 (see Map 2 on p. 137), where they agreed to co-operate in preventing disturbances in Macedonia from undermining the peace of the Balkans. The likelihood that the crisis in the far east might cause fundamental shifts in Russia's European policy began to be considered: perhaps the commitment to expansion in Asia and the possibility of war with Japan would lead the Russians to welcome a revived *Dreikaiserbund*; perhaps the failure of the French to support their ally would lead the Russians to abandon the alliance. The Germans encouraged these ideas and pushed them further along when, with the Russo-Japanese War raging in the far east, they signed a new commercial treaty with the Russians in July 1904.

The stage seemed set for a major shift in European diplomacy when ships in Russia's Baltic fleet, which had set out to make its way around Europe and Africa to join the fighting against Japan, fired on some British boats off the Dogger Bank (see Map 1 on p. 136). The Russians had mistaken some fishing boats for Japanese warships. Germany seized the opportunity to propose an alliance to Russia. They were to promise one another assistance against attack by an unspecified 'European power', which really meant that Germany would assist Russia against Britain and that Russia would assist Germany against France. The Germans even suggested that the Franco-Russian alliance need not be abandoned, as they imagined that it provided for the contingency of war against Britain, as well as against Germany. However, the Russians, in November 1904, refused the offer. There was to be no Russo-German equivalent of the Anglo-French entente.

The Germans, in spite of the apparently cautious terms they had suggested, were asking too high a price and had too little to offer in return. There were no Gambias or Madagascars in Russo-German relations. Even the idea of assistance against Britain could not be taken seriously: the German army was of no use against the empire; the German navy was in no condition to challenge the British. Some Germans even feared that the British would launch a preventive attack against the fleet that they were building, destroying the

German warships in harbour before they were strong enough to defend themselves [214]. The Germans could offer the Russians security on their western frontier, but neither Bülow nor Wilhelm II would be satisfied with a simple revival of the old Bismarckian arrangement, because this would have meant admitting that their policy had been a failure – and that Bismarck had been right when he had condemned the new course in German policy.

Any arrangement with Russia had to emphasise Germany's strength and the success of Bülow's 'world policy' [155; 195]. What the Germans were proposing in fact was their old idea of a 'continental league' with Germany at the centre, directing Russia and France. Bülow believed that recent events had shown that neither of them was able to act independently, or even, as the war with Japan had shown, together. But the negotiations conducted in the autumn of 1904 showed that Russia did not feel herself to be so weak as to compel her to join Germany. When the negotiations failed, Bülow, and the head of the political section in the German foreign ministry, Friedrich von Holstein, decided that they might be more successful in persuading the weaker member of the Dual Alliance, France, to join Germany. Bülow and Holstein were also anxious to show the French that their entente with the British was of little use to them when it came to a contest with Germany.

An opportunity almost exactly designed to fit German specifications came in January 1905 when a French mission arrived at Fez, the capital of Morocco. The aim of the mission was to institute a programme of internal reforms, and thus make it clear to the Moroccans that the French were in control [64; 304]. The Germans knew how deeply the French were committed to their ambitions in Morocco, for practically the entire French foreign ministry, and especially the bureaucrats of the Quai d'Orsay, aspired to establish a French empire there. When the sultan appealed to the Germans for assistance, therefore, they readily agreed. On 31 March, a somewhat reluctant Wilhelm II, who was about to embark upon a Mediterranean cruise, landed at Tangier with his entourage and rode through the streets in military uniform on a magnificent horse, with a band playing. When he reached the German legation he declared that he would support the continued independence of the Moroccan state. Germany, he announced, knew how to safeguard her interests.

But it was actually the absence of any significant German interest that gave this, the first Moroccan crisis, its peculiar character. The French had frequently approached the Germans over the previous decade with proposals for an arrangement concerning Morocco; Delcassé in particular believed that German assistance might be useful there in his diplomatic contest with Great Britain. The Germans always replied that they lacked sufficient interests in Morocco to become embroiled in a dispute [179]. Now, with the display of pomp and ceremony at Tangier, the Germans appeared to be suddenly reversing their position.

The point of the first Moroccan crisis, however, was not Morocco, but the nature of the relationship between Germany and France. If the French were forced to give in to German demands in an area where France had a significant interest and great plans for the future while Germany had few, it would make it plain that Germany was so much more powerful in Europe that France could expand her empire overseas only with Germany's consent [135]. It would mean nothing that the French navy was more powerful than the German, that the French army in Africa was more powerful than the German; in the future, all that would really matter would be the ability of Germany to defeat France on the ground in Europe. The Moroccan crisis was tremendously important because it seemed likely to determine whether or not France was still capable of pursuing an independent foreign policy.

It was this question of the future of France as a great power that drew Britain into the crisis. During the past decade, and especially since the kaiser's highly publicised telegram to Kruger in support of the Afrikaners at the outbreak of the Boer War, a group of young men had arisen within the British foreign office who were convinced that Germany posed a greater threat to the empire than did either Russia or France. This potential threat began to turn into something real with Germany's decision to construct an ocean-going navy. The 'germanophobes' of the foreign office argued that it was only the existence of France and Russia that kept German ambitions in check. These men, led by Francis Bertie [323], Arthur Nicolson [359], Charles Hardinge [364] and Eyre Crowe [338; 340], had, by the time of the first Moroccan crisis, achieved positions of authority. They were now convinced that if the French were forced to back down it would mean that France had been transformed into a satellite of Germany. In order to prevent this they argued that Britain must find some way to steady French nerves. They did not suggest that the entente had imposed this necessity on Britain; rather, it was precisely because the entente was not an alliance that they had to find, in the midst of the Moroccan crisis, some new way of assuring the French of British support.

Such assurance was forthcoming in May 1905, when the British foreign secretary, Lord Lansdowne, told the French ambassador in London, Paul Cambon, that Britain was prepared to transform the entente into an alliance. Lansdowne's words were vague but encouraging, as he suggested that Britain and France should 'discuss in advance any contingencies by which they might in the course of events find themselves confronted' [136]. In Paris, Delcassé argued that these words ought to be interpreted as the prelude to an alliance. But the French prime minister, Rouvier, believed that the Moroccan crisis might lead to war with Germany and that this would almost certainly end in another disastrous defeat for France. Hints of British assistance were not enough: even if it were forthcoming, how would it be made real? After all, the British navy 'does not run on wheels'.

When the Germans discovered what Delcassé was up to, they demanded that he be forced to resign. Rouvier agreed. The Germans thereby scored a great diplomatic victory: the architect of the Anglo-French entente had been forced out of office due to German pressure, and it appeared that France would no longer be capable of pursuing a foreign policy that did not meet with Germany's approval. The kaiser made von Bülow a prince, and Rouvier consented to Germany's insistence that an international conference be convened to settle the Moroccan dispute.

In the summer of 1905 everything seemed to be going Germany's way. Her success in Morocco was followed by the defeat of Russia in the far east. After a long and slow voyage from Europe, the Russian Baltic fleet had finally arrived off the coast of Japan in May 1905, where it was almost immediately destroyed. The battle of Tsushima on 27 May 1905 left Japan in absolute control of the sea. The Germans quickly renewed their efforts of the previous November to disengage Russia from her alliance with France. On 24 July the kaiser met the tsar at Björkö and persuaded him to sign a defensive alliance with Germany [128]. The success of the new course and world policy seemed guaranteed: French ambitions had been checked in Morocco, Russian strength sapped in the far east. Both states would now be forced to submit to German-directed alliances; Britain would be left in isolation.

Within three months of the meeting at Björkö however, it began to appear that Germany's success was less than complete. First, the tsar's closest advisers, the Grand Duke Nicholas Nikolayevich, Count Witte and Count Lambsdorff (the foreign minister), all joined in advising against an alliance with Germany, insisting that it would mean abandoning France, the end of the balance of power in Europe, and the encouragement of German expansion into the middle east. It was apparent to his advisers, if not to Nicholas II, that the 'defensive' arrangement proposed by the kaiser would reduce Russia to dependence on Germany. The proposed treaty of Björkö was therefore rejected in November. Secondly, the British decided that they would have to go further than Lansdowne's vague indications of support if the French will to resist German demands was to be bolstered. Accordingly, secret discussions with the French general staff were initiated in December 1905 in order to consider joint operations in the event of war [114; 336]. The British had implicitly recognised the validity of Rouvier's point concerning the uselessness of the royal navy to France: they would have to hold out the prospect of military assistance on the continent if critics of co-operation with Britain were to be satisfied [346; 354].

By the time the Morocco conference met at Algeciras in southern Spain on 16 January 1906, Germany's position had weakened considerably. Russia had chosen her alliance with France over the Björkö agreement; France had agreed to divide Morocco with Spain; and the new British foreign secretary, Sir Edward Grey, quickly showed that he was more suspicious of Germany – and therefore more inclined to support France – than his predecessor had been [153]. The conference showed that Germany could not even count on her allies.

The Italians, in December 1900, had secretly pledged to recognise the special interests of France in Morocco in exchange for a similar recognition of their rights in Libya. Two days after the Triple Alliance had been renewed in June 1902, the Italian foreign minister, Giulio Prinetti, signed a secret agreement with the French ambassador, Camille Barrère, that gave an assurance of Italian neutrality in any conflict into which France had been provoked. Prince von Bülow recognised, shortly after the conference convened, that Germany could not hope for a successful outcome: the only power sympathetic to her was Austria-Hungary – and even she counselled moderation. The final act of the conference, signed on 7 April 1906, although it affirmed Morocco's independence and integrity, left the policing of the country to France and Spain and gave the control of the *Banque d'État* to France, thereby placing her in a position to control Morocco's economic development [74; 233].

The débâcle of the Algeciras Conference had immediate repercussions within Germany. Holstein, the grey eminence of the foreign office who had done much to engineer the new course in

German policy, was forced to resign [187]. General von Moltke, who had succeeded von Schlieffen as chief of the general staff in January, proposed to alter his predecessor's plan for a war against France by providing for a pre-emptive strike through Belgium [185]. Admiral von Tirpitz, whose fleet-building scheme had been challenged in the autumn of 1905 by the British decision to begin constructing the huge new 'dreadnought' class of battleship, was now able to get the approval of the Reichstag* for an accelerated building programme of bigger ships in the Third Navy Law, which was ratified on 5 June 1906. A more general effect of the Moroccan crisis inside Germany was the widespread impression that she was being 'encircled', that the other European states resented her growing power and prosperity and would do everything they could to prevent her from assuming her rightful place as a world power. Germany, her leaders concluded, must rely less on diplomacy and more on her own military and naval strength.

There certainly seemed to be evidence to support the German belief that the ring around them was drawing tighter. Barely two weeks after the Algeciras Act was signed, the Russians agreed to a French proposal that the clauses in the Dual Alliance providing for military co-operation in a war against Great Britain should now be dropped. The French themselves had proposed these clauses in the aftermath of the Fashoda crisis of 1898; to drop them now indicated that they no longer regarded Britain as a possible enemy. Although there was still no Anglo-French alliance, these changes were significant because German policy since the accession of Wilhelm II had been predicated upon the assumption that Anglo-French and Anglo-Russian rivalry overseas would become increasingly bitter, and that this would work to Germany's advantage. Instead, the three powers showed signs that they might draw closer together: on 17 April France provided a huge new loan of 2,250,000,000 francs to Russia to shore up her disintegrating finances in the wake of the war against Japan [297]; in 1905 the British government decided to transfer ships from the Mediterranean – where they had been deployed to guard against France and Russia – to the North Sea [353]. The only possible interpretation of this move was that Britain was preparing for a challenge from the new German fleet. The question that remained unanswered was whether or not Britain and Russia would also find a way to resolve their differences.

In the midst of the Moroccan crisis an Anglo-Russian reconciliation seemed most unlikely. On 12 August 1905, Britain and Japan had agreed upon a revision of their alliance that extended its terms considerably and in a way highly unfavourable to Russia. First, it was extended geographically to include India and adjacent territories: the Japanese now promised to assist Britain if Russia attacked in central Asia. Secondly, the alliance would now operate if Russia attacked on her own: the provision for a two-power attack was dropped, so Russia, even without French assistance, would face combined British and Japanese forces should she become embroiled in a war with either of them [347].

The Russian failure in the far east, however, might render the revised Anglo-Japanese alliance insignificant. If Russia now decided to pursue a policy of caution in her relations with Britain and Japan, the new terms might never come into operation; and caution was made more likely by the moderate conditions of the Treaty of Portsmouth, which ended the Russo-Japanese War on 5 September 1905. In essence, all the treaty provided for was a Russian recognition of Japanese predominance in Korea and the withdrawal of Russian forces from southern Manchuria and south Sakhalin (see Map 3 on p. 138). These were hardly oppressive terms: there was no indemnity, and the Japanese public was far more disappointed than the Russian with the conditions of peace. There was no popular cry for revenge in Russia, no stimulus to further adventure. The 'Koreans', those in Russian governing circles who had argued that Russia's future lay in the far east, had been discredited by the disasters of the Russo-Japanese War. And, as the men in these circles had been generally 'pro-German', arguing that good relations with Germany on the western frontier gave Russia the safety necessary to expand in the far east and central Asia, the pro-German line of policy also suffered a setback.

But perhaps the most important effects of the war were its repercussions on the Russian political system. The war generated chaos and rebellion at home. The most famous incident occurred on 'Bloody Sunday' (22 January 1905) when the troops of the tsar opened fire on demonstrators, killing hundreds [282]. Not only did this discontent provide further impetus for a policy of restraint in foreign policy, it led to the signing of the October Manifesto on 30 October 1905, in which the tsar promised new civil rights, a Duma* (representative assembly) and a constitution. These promises were enacted in the 'Fundamental Laws' of 6 May 1906. Although the new system was still far from a parliamentary democracy, it did encourage the formation and circulation of public opinion; and most of this opinion, in the decade that followed, was unhappy with the idea of further imperialist adventures in Asia [276].

A new Russian foreign minister, A.P. Izvolsky, came into office in May 1906 eager to limit Russian commitments and to put relations with all the great powers on a more equable footing. Over the next seventeen months he managed to reach a political agreement with Japan (recognising her authority in Korea and southern Manchuria in exchange for her recognition of Russian authority in northern Manchuria and outer Mongolia), an agreement with Germany to maintain the *status quo* in the Baltic, and an agreement with Britain on Persia and Afghanistan. Izvolsky was seeking neither an alliance with Britain nor the encirclement of Germany. Rather, his policy aimed to provide stability and calm in Russia's foreign relations while the new political system took root and time healed the damage done by the war with Japan.

The Anglo-Russian agreement, which was signed on 31 August 1907, was even less of an alliance than the Anglo-French entente had been [72]. The two powers agreed that Tibet should act as a neutral buffer between their empires and that Russia should have no direct contact with Afghanistan. Thus, the British seemed to have achieved the security for their north-west frontier in India that they had long sought. Most difficult, and most important, was the agreement on Persia, which created a Russian sphere of influence in the more populous and richer north, and a British sphere in the south, bordering on Afghanistan and the Persian Gulf; a neutral sphere in the centre was to separate the two [329].

Like the Anglo-French entente, the Anglo-Russian version provided for no political action, no military planning, and suggested no possible contingencies that might lead the two powers to consult on these matters in the future. It was simply a resolution – and by no means a complete one – of long-standing differences that had made for troubled relations in central Asia [134; 320]. Like the Anglo-French entente, however, even this cautious arrangement threatened to undermine the foundations of German strategy, which had assumed that Britain and Russia would remain enemies and that this would eventually take one or the other of them into the German camp as a subordinate ally [165; 180].

6 THE VORTEX OF SOUTH-EASTERN EUROPE

With the Anglo-Japanese alliance and the end of the Russo-Japanese War in the far east, with the Anglo-French entente resolving differences in the Pacific, in North America, south-east Asia and Africa, and with the Anglo-Russian entente resolving differences in central Asia, it is not surprising that most diplomatic disputes in the following years were located in, or near, Europe itself [362]. This is not to suggest that Great Britain had carefully crafted a series of arrangements with old rivals in order to enable her to prepare for the inevitable conflict with imperial Germany. While it is true that some British officials felt threatened by German pretensions to world power, it is also true that practically nothing was done to transform the colonial ententes into European alliances. Moreover, the Russians, while they believed that the continued existence of France as an independent great power was essential to the balance of power and thus vital to their own security, did not believe that Germany posed any immediate danger to them. The 'diplomatic revolution' that took place between 1904 and 1907 thus represented a shift in mood and a change in emphasis; it did not represent the forging of a coalition that made war inevitable, or even predictable.

Many of those who participated in the diplomatic process believed the balance of power to be the best guarantee of peace, and that the rival alliance systems – with Britain remaining free to throw its weight on to either side – had established a better balance than had existed at any time since 1815. It was certainly arguable that the alliances had provided stability within Europe, where there had not been a significant crisis since the Russo-Turkish War of 1878 [84]. As important as the alliance system was to the maintenance of stability, south-eastern Europe remained one area where everyone continued to anticipate trouble; since 1897, however, the agreement between Russia and Austria-Hungary to put the Balkans 'on ice' had kept things quiet. The co-operation between the two powers had been extended in 1903 when, with a crisis brewing in Macedonia, their representatives had met at Murzsteg and agreed upon a programme of reforms that would preserve peace in the Balkans.

Ironically, it was this Austro-Russian co-operation in the Balkans that laid the groundwork for the first European crisis in thirty years. First, a new Austro-Hungarian foreign minister, Count Aehrenthal, came into office in 1906 determined to demonstrate that the differences between Vienna and Budapest did not mean that the Habsburg empire was finished as a great power. A recent political crisis had led some observers to argue that the empire was no longer capable of conducting a coherent foreign policy because of the differences between the Germans and the Magyars*. Aehrenthal decided that some of the problems that plagued the Dual Monarchy, especially those arising from questions of nationality, could be alleviated by a vigorous foreign policy [239]. The new chief of the general staff, Baron Conrad, supported Aehrenthal's view that the troublesome Serbs of southern Hungary could be silenced by reducing the independence and the pretensions of Serbia. The first step in this design would be to annex Bosnia and Herzegovina, the two autonomous provinces of the Ottoman empire, inhabited mainly by Serbs, that had been administered by Austria-Hungary since 1878. The annexation of the provinces would make it impossible for the Serbs to achieve their ambition of creating a large Serbian state that would incorporate all Serbs. The idea that nationalist agitation could be subdued by such a strategy was not particularly new; what was surprising was that the Russian foreign minister consented to it [71; 232].

Izvolsky was anxious to maintain the spirit of co-operation with the Austrians, but he also saw the possibility of achieving a diplomatic triumph that would bolster Russia's flagging prestige without putting her in any danger. When he met Aehrenthal at Büchlau, in Moravia, on 16 September 1908, he quickly became convinced that the Austrians were determined to occupy Bosnia and Herzegovina regardless of what the Russians might do. He concluded that to oppose the annexation would be dangerous, and, after the recent misadventure in the far east, to embark on such a dangerous course would be foolhardy. He proposed, instead, that in exchange for his acquiescence, Austria-Hungary should support Russia's long-standing ambition of having the Straits of the Bosphorus and the Dardanelles opened to the passage of warships in peacetime.

If the bargain had worked, Austro-Russian co-operation in the Balkans might have been maintained. But the Russian government refused to support Izvolsky, partly because public opinion, which was now more important under the new constitutional process, would be enraged by the abandonment of Slav brothers to Germanic rule. Izvolsky himself insisted that the Austrians, when they announced the annexation of the two provinces, had violated a number of the promises they had given him at Büchlau. On the other hand, the Austrians, led by the bellicose Conrad, were prepared to fight for the provinces, while the Russians were not. The German government supported Austria's policy, whereas France and Britain proved unwilling to join Russia in opposing it [116]. When, in February 1909, the Austrians threatened to invade Serbia unless Russia and Serbia formally recognised the annexation, the Russians felt that they had no choice but to comply. Negotiations to resolve the Bosnian situation in a spirit of co-operation ended in bitterness, suspicion and a renewed sense of rivalry [231].

The annexation crisis proved to be a turning-point in several significant ways [162]. First, it killed the Austro-Russian co-operation that had kept the Balkans reasonably quiet for the previous thirty years; from this point on the Balkans were in an almost constant state of turmoil. Secondly, it convinced Serbia that Austria-Hungary was aiming at her destruction as an independent state; from now on Serbian nationalists believed that they must rely on Russia for support and that, ultimately, only the break-up of the Dual Monarchy could save them. Finally, and most important, the Russians concluded that the unity between the Austrians and the Germans that had been demonstrated during the crisis posed a direct threat to them. Unlike their decision to proceed cautiously in the far east following the war with Japan, the Russians neither abandoned the Balkans nor came to an agreement with their antagonist. The Balkans and the Straits continued to be perceived as vital to Russia's security, to her reputation as a great power, and to her internal harmony. Accordingly, Russian ties with Serbia were tightened, mobilisation plans were refurbished, and a new programme of battleship-building in the Black Sea was launched [265].

The unfortunate Izvolsky was replaced in September 1910 by S.D. Sazonov. The new foreign minister apparently decided that, apart from strengthening the Russian presence in the Balkans, the best method of countering Austria-Hungary was to drive a wedge between her and Germany. His first visit was to Potsdam, where he agreed to drop Russian objections to German enterprises in the Ottoman empire and Persia in exchange for a promise that Germany would not support any form of Austrian aggression in the Balkans.

The Germans regarded the Bosnian crisis as convincing proof that neither the alliance with France nor the entente with Britain would provide Russia with any meaningful assistance in the Balkans [337]. Perhaps the ententes would prove equally useless to France in north Africa, where another crisis began to emerge in Morocco [65]. When demonstrators rioted in Fez against the rule of the sultan in the spring of 1911, French colonialists were encouraged to believe that the opportunity to impose direct French rule had come at last. In the foreign ministry the colonial party was firmly in control of policy: a weak minister, Jean Cruppi, who was ignorant of foreign affairs and incapable of countering arguments for intervention, ordered troops to Morocco on 17 April. By 21 May a joint Franco-Moroccan force of 20,000 had occupied Fez [64].

The French move violated both the Algeciras Act of 1906, which had left the Germans with some privileges in Morocco, and a Franco-German agreement of 1909 that recognised France's special political interests in Morocco in exchange for a promise that Germany's economic interests would not be damaged. These legal niceties counted for little, but they did provide the Germans with a legitimate excuse for responding to the French move. On the other hand, the German foreign minister, Alfred von Kiderlen-Wächter, whose ultimatum to Russia in the Bosnian crisis had proven to be such a dramatic success, privately believed that Morocco was bound to fall to the French sooner or later [125]. He decided to act not in order to protect German interests there but to demonstrate to the French that they were in no position to act unilaterally or to violate their agreements with Germany. The French would have to offer concessions before he would recognise their authority in Morocco; precisely what these were mattered little and Kiderlen had not defined them. On 1 July 1911 a German gunboat, *Panther*, steamed into the Moroccan port of Agadir, and the second Moroccan crisis began [211].

The British had not been pleased with the French decision to occupy Fez, which they interpreted as a triumph for the troublesome colonialists at the Quai d'Orsay [313]. When the Germans sent their gunboat to Agadir, however, the British quickly forgot their irritation with the French. The officials of the foreign office concluded that the Germans were not concerned to protect their interests in Morocco but were attempting to disrupt the entente by showing the French that they were too weak to resist German demands. The British feared that, unless they gave the French their support, they would be thrown into the 'teuton embrace' [319; 330]. Sir Edward

Grey was more cautious than the officials who advised him. He was prepared to countenance French concessions to Germany in the Congo in return for French control of Morocco; but even he began to worry when it appeared that the Germans were demanding almost all of the French Congo in exchange. Nevertheless, the cabinet, fearing that a strong line might lead to war, instructed Grey to inform the French that they would not regard as a legitimate cause of war a French decision to resist German territorial gains that might result from a settlement of the Moroccan crisis.

British actions during the crisis demonstrated that they, like the Germans, were not really concerned with territorial issues or economic privileges in either Morocco or the Congo. What worried them was that German power in Europe could be used to control French behaviour overseas; if this proved to be the result of the crisis, then France would be reduced to subordinate status and the balance of power in Europe would have shifted clearly in Germany's favour. In other words, Britain had no immediate fear of German imperialism, but she did regard the balance of power as essential to her security and she was increasingly concerned that this was being endangered by Germany. This thinking was quite different from that which had led to the entente with France in 1904 and explains why, on 21 July 1911, the chancellor of the exchequer, David Lloyd George, gave a strong speech at the Mansion House warning that Britain was not to be ignored in such matters [166; 339]. The Germans were offended by these strong words, and the British fleet was placed on alert.

Nevertheless, the crisis was resolved in October and November when the French conceded to the Germans two strips of territory in the Congo (amounting to some 100,000 square miles) in exchange for a recognition of the French protectorate in Morocco. This outcome pleased no one. The French colonialists, who had initiated the crisis, felt they had been abandoned by the British and by their own politicians; but they were themselves soon discredited [314]. A parliamentary inquiry into the handling of the crisis was instituted, which condemned the power of the officials at the Quai d'Orsay in its report [310]. Within a few months the chairman of the inquiry, Raymond Poincaré, had become premier and foreign minister. He was resolved to avoid any more colonial adventures and to work more closely with Russia and Britain. Grey, and his less moderate officials, felt that French impetuosity had brought them to the brink of war; although he believed that France must be supported in the event of a conflict with Germany, he was determined to restrain

French adventurism [342]. In Germany, Kiderlen had succeeded neither in subordinating France nor in driving a wedge into the entente; even the Congo concessions did not help him to save face. Where he had succeeded in the Balkans he failed in Morocco, and in Germany the general impression drawn from the crisis was that it was the wicked British who were pulling the strings of their French puppet. The British were determined to encircle Germany and prevent her natural development into a world power.

The only ones truly satisfied by the outcome of the Agadir crisis were the Italians. In a secret agreement signed in December 1900, they had recognised the special interests of France in Morocco in return for recognition of their special interests in the Ottoman provinces of Tripolitania and Cyrenaica (Libya) (see Map 4 on p. 139). When the French moved into Fez, the Italians began to consider a similar move into Tripoli. Public support for such a move was widespread and enthusiastic; the government, in fact, was more cautious than the people. But the Italians had also prepared the diplomatic ground more carefully than the French: in March 1902 Britain had recognised Italy's special interests in Libya, and in October 1909 Russia had been persuaded to do the same. The Italians assumed that they could also count on the support of Germany and Austria-Hungary, their partners in the Triple Alliance [255]. On 20 September the Italian government decided to invade Libya, believing that the war would be short and simple; but, as so often proved to be the case, this forecast was unduly optimistic [257]. The Libyan campaign lasted more than a year and formal recognition of the Italian annexation did not come until after the First World War [241; 245].

Although no power opposed Italy's invasion of Libya, neither did anyone give her their enthusiastic support, least of all her partners in the Triple Alliance [228; 333]. Conrad, the chief of the Austrian general staff, went so far as to propose taking advantage of Italy's commitment in Africa by attacking her in the north – a daring plan that was rejected by the politicians. Once again, none of the European powers were really concerned with Libya itself; what concerned them were the repercussions that the Italian invasion might have throughout the rest of the Ottoman empire. There was a growing belief in all the European capitals that the empire was in danger of dissolution, which would raise a series of extremely complicated questions, as the near east was the one area where all six great powers had interests and ambitions [66; 302].

The British in particular worried that this succession of crises in the Mediterranean would lead to war, if current trends continued. One of the factors that seemed to be pointing to war by 1911 was the Anglo-German naval race [173]. It would be quite wrong to assume, however, that the British immediately interpreted the German decision to build a navy as a threat to the empire. In spite of the German naval bills of 1898 and 1900, the British government continued to calculate its naval requirements on the basis of the two-power standard of France and Russia [208]. Only when the Russian fleet was destroyed by the Japanese did the British admiralty propose to substitute Germany for Russia in their calculations. Even then the change did not signify a political decision to view Germany as the emerging enemy, but was rather a continuation of the long-standing policy of the admiralty to prepare to fight simultaneously Britain's two strongest rivals, in case they should then combine with one another. At the time of the first Moroccan crisis no one believed that Germany, on her own, would be able to match the British navy, and no one believed in the possibility of a Franco-German alliance. The decisive change came when the British concluded that Germany was aiming to establish her hegemony in Europe, the first stage of which would be the domination of France. Only then did Germany begin to be seen as Britain's principal rival, and this for continental political reasons, not imperial and naval ones [210; 349].

In 1905, British planners began to construct contingency plans for war against Germany – long before the German fleet was seen as a serious threat to British security. The plans were designed to provide France with assistance in the event of a German attack, which explains why the Committee of Imperial Defence* decided, during the Moroccan crisis, that an expeditionary force should be created that would be capable of fighting on the continent itself. From 1905 on, additional changes in strategy were instituted in order to meet the German threat: more of the fleet was concentrated in home waters, new battleship-building paralleled that of Germany. By 1911 everyone spoke of the Anglo-German naval 'race' and some believed that it was the real cause of the antagonism between the two countries that brought them close to war during the Agadir crisis [81].

When the minister of war, Viscount Haldane, was sent on a special mission to Germany in February 1912, therefore, some members of the government hoped that an end to the naval race could be negotiated and that this would diminish the growing sense of an impending conflict. But the mission failed. On the eve of his arrival, new and more ambitious navy and army bills were announced in the Reichstag [212]; and, in the negotiations that followed, the Germans insisted that the first step in any naval agreement must be a British promise of neutrality in the event of war [160]. The German moves merely served to convince Sir Edward Grey that his fears were justified, that Germany was indeed aiming to neutralise Britain in order to dominate France [82]. He concluded that only strong British support would enable France to remain independent, but he also steadfastly refused to turn this support into an alliance. Grey feared that, if Britain went too far in her assurances, it would encourage French adventurism.

His fear was probably no longer justified after Poincaré, who aimed to subdue the adventurers in the Quai d'Orsay, became premier of France in January 1912. Poincaré believed that the colonialists had taken France to the brink of disaster in the Agadir crisis; he preferred a policy of caution and stability, and the best guarantee of stability, he believed, was to be found in the balance of power that had been established with the alliance system. France, he said, should be a firm and loyal ally of Russia, draw as close as possible to Britain and avoid the temptation of working to disrupt the Triple Alliance, either by an agreement with Italy or with Germany.

This policy, which was apparently safer and more straightforward, was potentially more dangerous than that of Poincaré's predecessors. No longer would France fail to support Russia in the Balkans. In September 1912, he assured the Russians that, if a crisis in the Balkans led to war with the Central Powers, they could count on the French fulfilling their obligations to assist them [115; 264]. In giving this commitment to the Russians, Poincaré was relying largely upon Izvolsky's personal reputation for caution and moderation.

But there were other, less cautious, forces at work within Russia and in the Balkans. The Italian war with Turkey had encouraged the Balkan states in general, and Serbia and Bulgaria in particular, to anticipate the final dissolution of the Ottoman empire in Europe [275; 277]. This would at last make it possible for them to incorporate into their states the Serbs and Bulgars who remained in the Turkish province of Macedonia. Although Serbia and Bulgaria had long been bitter rivals, two Russian ambassadors, Hartwig in Serbia and Neklyudov in Bulgaria, succeeded in encouraging them to overcome their differences and to come together in the spirit of Slavic brotherhood. A Serbo-Bulgarian alliance was signed in March, 1912 [140]. Within a few months a complicated network of alliances and alignments had been constructed, linking Greece and Montenegro with Serbia and Bulgaria in a 'Balkan League' [156]. In spite of the efforts of both Russia and Austria-Hungary to restrain them, the Montenegrins declared war on Turkey on 8 October 1912 and the other Balkan states quickly followed them. The Turks were defeated rather easily in the Balkans, although the Bulgarian attack on Constantinople became bogged down in the mud [167; 268].

The defeat of the Turks suited neither the Austrians nor the Russians. An expanded Serbia, with a coastline on the Adriatic, would prove an even more troublesome neighbour for Austria-Hungary, encouraging the growth of Serbian nationalism within the Dual Monarchy. A big Bulgarian state in possession of Constantinople would be in a position to inflict serious damage on Russia, especially if the Bulgarians continued to co-operate with the Austrians. The two great powers informed the Balkan states, therefore, that no change in the *status quo* would be permitted without their consent, and a conference of ambassadors met in London in December 1912 to sort things out [73].

The general principle adopted at the London conference was that the Turks should lose their remaining possessions in Europe, except for a rump of land around the Dardanelles and Bosphorous Straits stretching from Enos to Midia (see Map 5 on p. 140). This satisfied Russia because it kept the Bulgarians away from this strategically sensitive area. The conference also agreed that an independent state should be created in Albania. This satisfied Austria-Hungary because it limited Serbian gains to a restricted area in the interior. Both great powers had feared that the war would upset the balance in the Balkans and that their potential enemies would be placed in a better position to threaten them than they had been previously. But diplomacy, in this instance, had triumphed. Russia and Austria-Hungary had proved reluctant to champion the cause of their satellites, Serbia and Bulgaria; the continuing rivalry among the Balkan states themselves enabled the great powers to impose a settlement upon them. The 'preliminaries of peace' were signed in London on 31 May 1913 [122].

War broke out again in less than a month. The Bulgarians felt that they had been cheated of a proper victory in the First Balkan War because the Serbs and Greeks had occupied, and retained, territories that ought to have gone to them. At the end of June, therefore, Bulgaria attacked Serbia, and the Second Balkan War was underway. The Greeks immediately joined in against the Bulgarians; so too did the Rumanians and the Turks. Faced with this coalition,

Bulgaria was easily defeated and, by the end of July, she was ready to come to terms. The Treaty of Bucharest, signed on 11 August 1913, expanded the territories of Serbia, Greece and Rumania; a further Treaty of Constantinople, signed on 30 September 1913, permitted Turkey to recover some of the territory she had earlier lost to Bulgaria [86].

The Balkan Wars left a dangerous legacy in the Balkans [83]. The victors, now bigger and more powerful, nevertheless remained dissatisfied. Serbia, which had doubled in size, was still landlocked and made plain its sympathy with the Serbs of Austria-Hungary, whom it regarded as oppressed brethren. Greece, which had expanded to take in almost all territories where Greek was the language of the majority, looked beyond her frontiers to a 'greater Greece' that included Constantinople and substantial portions of Asia Minor. Austria-Hungary and Turkey had good reason to believe that new dangers lay ahead [144]. And Bulgaria, not surprisingly, was embittered by the disasters of the previous year – she had lost 25,000 men and been brought to the verge of revolution; she would eagerly grasp any opportunity that offered her a chance to reverse the outcome of 1913 [238].

In spite of the success of Serbia and the failure of Bulgaria, Russia too was dissatisfied with the experience of the Balkan Wars. First, at decisive moments of crisis, the Austrians had managed to impose their views by threatening war against Serbia and Montenegro. Secondly, the Germans showed increasing signs of committing themselves to an ambitious policy in the middle east both by supporting Austria-Hungary in the Balkans and by turning Turkey into a satellite [199; 230]. One of the most consistent elements in the policy of Wilhelm II had been the encouragement of German interests in the middle east, and by 1914 Germany was the most important foreign component in the Turkish economy [77; 121]. Even more worrying in Russian eyes was the appointment of a German general, Liman von Sanders, to command the Turkish garrison at Constantinople. If this permitted Germany to control the Straits, in a moment of crisis it could place Russia in a very difficult position, as more than one-third of her trade moved between the Black Sea and the Mediterranean [218]. By 1914 it had become an axiom of Russia's policy that, although there was no compelling need for her to seize Constantinople for herself, she would fight rather than allow a foreign power to do so [*Doc. 10*] [280].

Russia's fears of German ambitions in the middle east were not unjustified [193]. In the autumn of 1913 Wilhelm II had assured both the chief of the general staff and the foreign minister of Austria-Hungary that the time for decisive military action in the Balkans was drawing near and that Germany could be relied upon for support. In February 1914 Russian military intelligence intercepted two German memoranda that expressed determination to capture Constantinople should the Ottoman empire collapse, and that suggested ways to prepare German public opinion for the coming war with Russia and France. These revelations convinced the Russians that a combined Austro-German effort would soon be made to establish predominance in the Balkans and at the Straits. They replied to this threat by consolidating their relationship with France and Britain and by relying upon Serbia – with her army of 200,000 men and 200,000 reservists – to act as the bastion against further Austrian expansion [309].

Ironically, considering these Russian fears, the Austrians and the Germans had reason to believe that their situation was deteriorating. The success of the Schlieffen plan, and Moltke's revision of it in 1911, depended upon the ability of Austro-German forces to keep Russia at bay in the east while the Germans knocked out the French in the west; the German strategists believed that this was the only method by which they could hope to win a two-front war. The role that had been assigned to Austria-Hungary was an offensive one: she was to launch an attack through Galicia, which would force a significant part of the Russian army to stand on the defensive [161]. But this scheme had been designed before the Balkan Wars and before the growing size and power of Serbia placed in doubt some of the strategic assumptions on which it was based. The latest estimates were that Austria-Hungary would have to commit half of her forces to the south if a crisis began there [75]. At the same time as the threat of Serbia was growing in the south, Russian military strength appeared to be expanding rapidly. A 'Great Military Programme' had been adopted in November 1913 that provided for a 40 per cent increase in the size of the standing army over the next four years. The expansion in the number of troops available to Russia was to be supplemented by continuing with the rapid expansion of the railway network, an expansion that was made possible by a combination of French loans and the industrial revolution that was going on in the Ukraine [273; 312].

Wilhelm II's apparently wild encouragement to the Austrians to settle the Serbian question once and for all was, therefore, not as irrational as it might appear [206]. If the danger in the south were removed, Austria-Hungary could again concentrate her forces against Russia, and the foundations of the Schlieffen plan would be restored. Thus, on 28 June 1914, when a Serbian nationalist in Sarajevo assassinated the Austrian successor to the throne during his visit to Bosnia, a situation seemed to have presented itself that was tailor-made to suit German requirements: Austria-Hungary could 'settle' the Serbs, who were unlikely to receive much support, given the facts of the assassination. Neither France nor Britain had ever demonstrated an inclination to support Russia's Balkan policy in the past [*Doc. 12*] [69].

When, on 4 July, the emperor Franz Joseph wrote to Wilhelm II that he proposed to 'eliminate Serbia as a power factor in the Balkans' he received a sympathetic response. After consulting his chancellor, Bethmann Hollweg, the kaiser urged Austria-Hungary to make war on Serbia, issuing what has long been referred to as the 'blank cheque' in assuring the Austrians of support – even if this meant going to war with Russia [*Doc. 11*] [177; 182]. But the kaiser did not believe that Russia would intervene, for this would require the tsar to come out in support of assassins, which seemed a most unlikely position for any monarch to take. Wilhelm therefore saw no need to alter his summer vacation plans and proceeded to leave on a cruise. No preparations for war were made. Bethmann Hollweg foresaw the disintegration of the Triple Entente [192]. The Germans believed that they had a great diplomatic victory in their grasp [205; 236].

Speed was essential to such a victory. Austria-Hungary would have to act quickly and decisively to present Serbia with a *fait accompli* while the memory of the assassination was still vivid [240]. But the Austrians did not move quickly, as the politicians proved to be badly divided on the next step to be taken: the foreign minister, Berchtold, proposed to launch a surprise attack, while the Hungarian prime minister, Count Tisza, insisted that some diplomatic preparation was necessary if Austria-Hungary was not to be branded as an aggressor [222]. Tisza proposed to issue a list of stiff, but not impossible, demands, which, if accepted, would give Austria-Hungary almost everything she needed without resorting to war [237]. The rest of the ministers agreed on 7 July to the idea of presenting Serbia with a series of demands; they also agreed that there should be no mobilisation until these demands had been rejected and an ultimatum issued [234]. On the other hand, they also agreed that the demands should be so extreme as to make it virtually impossible for the Serbs to agree to them. The Austrian strategy slowed down the process so much that it practically negated the original German plan. The note containing the demands and the ultimatum was not presented until 23 July – almost three weeks after the blank cheque had been issued [*Doc. 15*] [223; 228].

When the Russian foreign minister, Sazonov, received a copy of the demands on the following day he immediately concluded that the Austrians knew they would be unacceptable and that they must therefore have been designed as a prelude to war with Serbia. He also believed that the Austrians would not have gone this far had they not been certain of German support. At a council of ministers on 24 July Sazonov maintained that, if Serbia were abandoned to Austria-Hungary, Russia's position in the Balkans would 'collapse utterly'. Furthermore, as the crisis was being used by the Germans to increase their power in central Europe and in the middle east, Russia would, if she failed to take a strong stand, come to be seen as a decadent state and slip into the ranks of the second-rate powers [264]. The defence ministers, although they could not guarantee a military victory over Germany and Austria-Hungary, argued that there was no military reason why Russia should not display firmness in diplomatic negotiations [272]. That evening Serbia was given an assurance of Russia's continuing support.

It is questionable whether Russia would have responded so decisively had she not been confident of French support. Poincaré, however, had insisted upon the closest possible connection with Russia as the most vital ingredient of his foreign policy. He had decided, in contrast with the Bosnian crisis of 1908, that France could not jeopardise that alliance with Russia by once again failing to support her in the Balkans; if Russia were forced to yield in the Balkans it would encourage the pro-German group at St Petersburg to insist on a reconciliation with Germany [298]. If Russia were reconciled to Germany, if the French alliance with Russia were dissolved, the balance of power in Europe would be destroyed and France would no longer be capable of acting as an independent great power [271; 286].

Because the Russians hoped to avoid a confrontation with Germany, they attempted to limit the escalation of the crisis to a contest between themselves and the Austrians. When, therefore, on 24–25 July, they undertook military measures preliminary to a mobilisation, they attempted to localise the crisis by preparing to mobilise only in the military districts of Odessa, Kiev, Kazan and Moscow. In this way they hoped to demonstrate their determination to intervene if Austria-Hungary attacked Serbia, but at the same time to avoid the appearance of a challenge to Germany.

Any lingering doubts there may have been in Russia concerning Austria's intentions disappeared when the Austrians rejected the Serbian reply to their demands. The Serbs had gone much further in the attempt to accommodate Austria-Hungary than the Russians, the French and the British had believed possible [226]. On 28 July, the day after she received the Serbian reply, Austria-Hungary declared war on Serbia; the next day Belgrade was shelled. On 30 July, the Russian government, convinced by the military authorities that a partial mobilisation was impossible, ordered a general mobilisation [*Doc. 16*] [283].

The German military authorities had by this time come round to the view that, as war seemed likely, and as Austria-Hungary could not be abandoned if she were to fight Russia, this was probably the best opportunity they would have for a contest with the entente [184]. The French, they argued, were not prepared for a fight, while the Russians would only continue to grow stronger with each passing year [94]. Moltke was convinced that, even if the British did enter the war (and it was far from certain that they would), the French could still be beaten quickly and decisively; the 150,000 men of the British expeditionary force would make no difference [316]. The Russian mobilisation played directly into the hands of the militarists: they were now able to argue that if Germany failed to respond to it immediately her long-standing strategic plans would be negated [95]. Moreover, because Russia had taken the initiative, the German people as a whole would support the war effort. On the morning of 31 July, therefore, Germany mobilised and insisted that Russia cease all military measures aimed at Germany and Austria-Hungary within twelve hours. No reply came. Germany declared war on Russia at 6 p.m. on 1 August [183].

The most fateful step had been taken. Once Germany declared war on Russia, France had little choice but to join in. Not to have done so would have signalled that she was finished as a great power. This was made abundantly clear on 1 August when the Germans asked what the French attitude would be in the event of a Russo-German war – while telling the French that, should they choose to remain neutral, they would have to surrender the fortresses on their eastern frontier. The Germans were determined to be the winners, and to be seen to win, whether or not they met the French on the field of battle. The French replied to these demands by announcing their mobilisation. Two days later Germany declared war on France; on 4 August she invaded Belgium.

An awful sense of predetermination surrounds the events of the

first days of August: each step along the road to war from the
Austrian ultimatum onwards appears, in hindsight, to have been
logical and irreversible. But this could not be foreseen prior to the
events. Italy, for example, was not drawn into the abyss as a result
of her prior commitments. On 3 August she declared her neutrality
[260]. Her partners in the Triple Alliance had practically ignored
her during the crisis, mainly because they distrusted her, but also
because they had a low opinion of her abilities as a great power.
They offered her nothing in exchange for honouring her commitments. Thus, if Italy had chosen to side with Germany and Austria-
Hungary in spite of these snubs, she would have confirmed her role
as a weak and subordinate member of the alliance, and could expect
to be treated as such in the future. The Italians, calmly and
rationally, chose to remain on the sidelines and wait upon events.

Although the British reached a different conclusion, they too
refused to be drawn into the war as if their participation had been
predetermined. As the crisis unfolded, Grey made it clear to Russia
and France that Britain was entirely free from commitments [334].
In spite of repeated efforts to include Britain in a demonstration of
entente solidarity, Grey feared that such a demonstration would
alarm the Germans and deepen the crisis; he counselled moderation
and direct negotiations between Russia and Austria-Hungary. Even
when the Austrians presented their ultimatum, the seriousness of
which Grey fully recognised, and then spurned the Serbian reply,
Grey refused to take any dramatic steps. His advisers at the foreign
office were distressed: from the time of the ultimatum onward they
were convinced that the crisis was being used by Germany to
achieve her ambition of political domination in Europe. On the
other hand, the foreign secretary kept those members of the cabinet
who were known to be opposed to any British armed intervention in
the dark concerning the details of the crisis and the expectations of
support in France and Russia [344].

Grey was determined to avoid a conflict if at all possible, but he
also believed that Britain would have to assist France if she went to
war with Germany. In the last days of July he began to prepare the
cabinet for the worst. Germany, he warned, did not seem interested
in mediation and appeared to be doing nothing to restrain
Austria-Hungary. On 29 July the majority of the cabinet refused to
agree to his proposal that they should promise to support France;
they even refused to promise to uphold the neutrality of Belgium
that had been guaranteed by treaty in 1839 [139]. If Belgian
neutrality were violated, they decided, the British decision would be

'one of policy rather than legal obligation'. On 1 August Grey was forced to tell the French ambassador that a British expeditionary force might not be sent to France, even if Britain were to enter the war. On the next day, following a plea from the French government, the cabinet did agree to warn the Germans that Britain would not tolerate any naval action by them in the English Channel or on the French coast; but the Germans readily assented to this provision.

The British decision to present this ultimatum to the Germans was significant, nevertheless, because a large majority of the cabinet had finally agreed that they had to support the entente. The only question that remained after 2 August was what form this support ought to take. One minister, John Burns, resigned; the others who had earlier opposed intervention now realised that if they forced the issue, the government would fall, probably to be replaced by a coalition that would intervene anyway [366; 368].

The violation of Belgian neutrality by Germany on 4 August provided a convenient justification for those in the British cabinet who had already reluctantly decided that intervention was inevitable. They could now claim to have supported war for reasons of morality and law. Britain's entry into the war had little to do with Belgium; if Germany had not invaded there might have been a few more resignations, but nothing more. Britain would have intervened in any case, believing that this was essential to preserve the balance of power and prevent the German domination of Europe [*Doc. 14*]. On 6 August it was agreed to send the expeditionary force to France. Within a week the five great powers were at war.

PART FOUR: ASSESSMENT

The most persistent assumption underlying the decisions of July 1914 was the illusion that the war would be short [175]. The thinking behind this was relatively simple: modern methods of transportation and communication created unprecedented opportunities for speed and mobility in attack. This lesson had been learned in the Franco-Prussian War of 1870. The Prussian use of railways had been decisive; the French, after all, had had as many men under arms and were, in every measurable military category, as powerful as the Germans. The difference, it was believed, was to be found in the Prussian ability to harness the new possibilities for warfare to be found in industrial society. The lessons that might have been learned from the Russo-Japanese War and the Balkan Wars had been discounted accordingly: they had not been fought by peoples or in regions to which the new technology applied. All the war plans of the great powers before 1914 hinged on railway timetables and the rapid deployment of men in the field.

The belief in speed was crucial. The most famous stratagem, the Schlieffen plan, called for a lightning attack on France's western flank – but this was not exceptional; in France, Joffre proposed a quick strike through Alsace in his Plan 17* [317]; in Russia, Plan B* called for Russia to seize the offensive and attack through Poland; in Austria-Hungary, the alliance with Germany provided for an attack on Russia to be launched from Galicia; in Great Britain, the planning for the British Expeditionary Force assumed that it must land in France within days of a war being declared in order for it to be effective. These plans showed the extent to which strategists had committed themselves to the view that standing on the defensive would lead to ruin [219; 321]. The Germans believed that they had to defeat France quickly to enable them to concentrate their full attention on Russia, and that an Austrian offensive against Russia would be vital in allowing them time to defeat France. The Russians believed that only an overwhelming attack in the east could prevent the Germans from overrunning France in the west [89; 301].

Although most of these strategic calculations turned out to be mistaken, they were essential to the decisions made at the end of July and the beginning of August. Once the first steps towards mobilisation were taken, everyone assumed that it would be fatal to stand still while their potential enemies moved forward. The most important steps were the Russian mobilisation and the German response to it. When the Russians attempted to mobilise against Austria-Hungary alone, they discovered that this was practically impossible, as they had made no plans for such a contingency and lacked the logistical support to carry it out. Moreover, beginning with a partial mobilisation would make a general one extremely difficult, should it prove impossible to localise the war in the Balkans [112]. If the Germans had permitted the Russian mobilisation to be carried through without responding in kind, it would have jeopardised what was regarded as their only feasible plan for fighting a major war. By 28–30 July the generals had taken over from the politicians and the nature of their plans made a general war among the great powers a virtual certainty [106; 163].

It is also true that Germany had really decided to force a war before Russia mobilised. Although the war plans are important in understanding why the crisis unfolded in the way that it did, they provide only a partial answer to the question, 'why did the war begin?' Ultimately, the German decision to force a war with Russia was not determined so much by railway timetables as by their belief that they could not permit Austria-Hungary to be defeated, and that if a war for the future of the Balkans and the middle east had to be fought some time, the best time was now [111]. It is tempting, given this Austro-German connection on the one hand, and the Franco-Russian on the other, to regard the alliance 'system' as the real cause of the war.

The system, however, worked far from systematically in July 1914. First, Italy refused to come to the assistance of her allies. Germany and Austria-Hungary alike distrusted her and kept her in the dark when critical decisions were being made [164; 259]. The Triple Alliance turned out not to be a Triplice after all. Nor did the 'Triple Entente' operate as an alliance. No one, not the Russians, not the French, not the Central Powers, knew what Britain's response to the crisis would be. The Russian decision to mobilise was taken in spite of the absence of any guarantee of support from the British; the German decision to force a war with Russia was taken when the attitude of the British was still uncertain. The British case shows that not all of the great powers were committed to act; the Italian case shows that even when commitments existed these could be ignored if it seemed to be in someone's interest to ignore them. It was not the alliance 'system' that drew the great powers into war in 1914, but the belief that it was more dangerous to stay out of a war than enter into one [127; 261].

Each of the great powers decided in 1914 that they had vital interests at stake, interests for which it was worth risking defeat, dismemberment, impoverishment and social revolution. Had they anticipated the extent of the carnage, the duration of the war, the political and social chaos that it caused, they might have made different decisions. But even this is doubtful. By and large the men who made the decisions, drawn mainly from the traditional ruling classes of Europe, believed it better to die honourably than to survive in disgrace – and this applied to their states as well as to themselves [*Doc. 13*]. This was especially true of the eastern powers, Austria-Hungary, Russia and Germany, who felt that they were already teetering on the brink of a disaster, and that war (which they hoped and assumed would be successful) was the only alternative to a humiliating diplomatic defeat [152; 345].

A more difficult question is why, when the great powers had survived a succession of crises over the previous decade, this one led to a general war. What distinguished the July crisis from the first and second Moroccan crises, or from the First and Second Balkan Wars? The war plans and the system of alliances had not differed in any fundamental way; the real difference was the fact that in these earlier crises one or more of the leading participants took the view that the interests at stake did not justify the risk of war. Nor would it have been easy to persuade people to take up arms on behalf of some of the issues involved in these crises. Few Germans were convinced that the economic stake in Morocco was worth a war with France; few Russians could have been persuaded that the change from an Austrian occupation of Bosnia and Herzegovina to a protectorate was worth fighting to stop. The crisis of July 1914 was exceptional in that the issues at stake made it possible for each of the great powers to mobilise public support, without which war would have been impossible.

The first fateful step along the road to war was taken by Austria-Hungary when her government decided that the assassination at Sarajevo at last gave her the opportunity she had been looking for to 'solve' the problem of Slav nationalism – a problem that was seen to threaten her continued existence. Such an opportunity was not likely to come again. Although the actual extent of complicity on the part of Serbian officials was not known at the time, all of the great powers expected Austria-Hungary to take some action against Serbia, and they accepted this as justified. Each of the 'entente' powers urged Serbia to be as accommodating as possible when she replied to the Austrian ultimatum – and they would have accepted the considerable limitations on her independence that her reply involved. Moreover, the assassination provided more than a pretext: it offered a possibility of mobilising public sentiment throughout the Dual Monarchy in favour of vigorous action; any future attempt to 'solve' the Slav problem was unlikely to occur in such favourable circumstances. Finally, Germany's strong encouragement to act decisively and crush the Serbian threat once and for all was decisive: her support had been essential in the Bosnian crisis of 1909, and without it Austria-Hungary would not have dared to risk war with Russia. Thus, it may be legitimately argued that a substantial underlying cause of the war was nationalism in general, and in particular the demand for unified, independent states in the Balkans and the threat this posed to the socio-political structure of Austria-Hungary [229].

But there would not have been a war in 1914 if Russia had declined to support Serbia. Her fateful decision to mobilise on Serbia's behalf (even if only partially at first) was made at several different levels. First, the strategic calculation was that Russia could not permit the transformation of Serbia into a satellite of Austria-Hungary because this would lead to an Austrian domination of the Balkans which, when combined with Germany's expanding role in Turkey, might allow the Central Powers to dominate most of the middle east. If Austria-Hungary and Germany dominated the Balkans and the Straits it would make the defence of Russia extremely difficult and endanger vital Russian trade. Secondly, support for the Slavic peoples of south-eastern Europe was the one programme that tied together almost all sections of influential Russian society. Whereas the war against Japan had been popular with only a few, and whereas a war against Britain in central Asia would have stirred up little emotional support, almost all sectors of the Russian political community believed that Russia was destined to perform a great cultural and religious task in south-eastern Europe. In fact, the Russian government would have been severely shaken by opposition had it failed to respond forcefully to Austria-Hungary's ultimatum. Thirdly, in contrast with 1909, the French had assured the Russians that they would support them in the Balkans, and it was highly unlikely that, if the Russians now backed down and allowed the Central Powers to prevail, such support would again be available in the future. Thus, it may be argued that the Russian version of Slav nationalism was an underlying cause of the war because, had the government abandoned what was widely perceived to be its historical mission, the cultural foundations of the tsarist state might have been shaken too badly for it to survive.

The July crisis was, in essence, an Austro-Russian one; the transformation of that crisis into a world war was the responsibility of Germany [157; 158]. The German government decided immediately following the assassination that the perfect opportunity had arisen by which Austria-Hungary could eradicate much of the internal unrest that plagued her while simultaneously reducing the Balkans to an order that suited Austro-German interests. This was not a decision calculated to precipitate a war but rather one which looked forward to a diplomatic triumph even more dramatic than that of 1909. The triumph that the Germans envisioned in the summer of 1914 would strengthen Austria-Hungary while attaching her to Germany even more closely in the future. The fateful moment came when Russia undertook a partial mobilisation, which made it clear that she would not back down this time. Faced with this determined Russian response, Germany had either to go backward, by restraining her ally and admitting to another defeat in diplomacy, or go forward by threatening Russia with a general war. She chose to go forward [169; 176].

The thinking behind Germany's decision was both strategic and political. Her military leaders advised that her position relative to Russia would deteriorate over the next few years. The Russian army would be expanded at a rate that Germany could not hope to match; the Russian economy appeared to have passed through the first stages of an industrial revolution; plans for railway construction, if they were realised, would allow the Russians to maximise the advantage they enjoyed in their numbers of fighting men [185]. Politically, German leaders concluded that they had been 'encircled' by Russia, France and Great Britain, and that the decade-long series of diplomatic crises had demonstrated that it was impossible to break this combination by peaceful means [137; 217]. The German landowners and the bourgeoisie were also generally inclined to believe that a great victorious war would enable them to triumph over those elements in German society, particularly the socialists of the industrial cities, who were opposed to their continuing domination of the German state. The most significant of the underlying causes of the war was the dynamic growth of German power in the decades that preceded it, and the fact that the management of that power resided with an elite who had come to believe that war was an attractive policy because it usually brought them social, political and economic rewards [90].

The German, Russian and Austrian decisions were the momentous ones. Given Moltke's revision of the Schlieffen plan, France was bound to be attacked, no matter what she did. Her only alternative to fighting was to concede defeat in advance. But the role of France was significant nevertheless. Had Russia not been repeatedly assured by Poincaré, since he came to power in 1912, of French assistance in any future Balkan crisis, she might have been more reluctant to support Serbia to the point of war with Austria-Hungary. Furthermore, without the Russian alliance, which almost all France's statesmen regarded as indispensable to her foreign policy, it is possible that the Schlieffen plan would not have been formulated. But the French believed that without the Russian alliance there would be no balance of power and France would inevitably succumb to the domination of Germany [298]. Although the French decision to go to war, therefore, was not made on the basis of *revanche* for the 'lost provinces' of Alsace and Lorraine, national pride was significant in encouraging French politicians to fight for France's survival as an independent great power [292; 303].

Cwt of AL

Of the five great powers that went to war in August 1914, Britain played the least significant part. Her support, or lack of it, neither encouraged nor restrained Russia and France. While some have argued that war might have been averted if she had made it evident early in the crisis that she would assist Russia and France in the event of a general European war, this seems doubtful. The German military – as well as the French – took little account of Britain's ability to contribute substantially to the fighting; their plans hinged on a quick knock-out blow of France, and they assumed that this would have been achieved before Britain could do much about it. Had the Germans anticipated a four-year-long war of attrition they would perhaps have rated British power more highly. It might just as easily be argued that if Britain had taken a strong and committed line from the start she would simply have confirmed the argument of those Germans who believed that she was behind the policy of encirclement, and that an armed conflict was the only way whereby Germany could break up the coalition that had been organised to contain her.

The British, who had done their best in the decade before 1914 to show the French that they would stand by them if they were threatened by Germany, consistently refused to commit themselves in advance of events [137]. This was not due to Liberal fuzzy-mindedness or adherence to tradition, but to a realistic appraisal of the situation on the continent. The British rated themselves more highly than the Germans did; consequently, they believed that if the French and/or the Russians were guaranteed British support in a war they would be more intransigent in times of crisis and might even provoke a conflict. The British were nevertheless drawn reluctantly into the war in August 1914 because they believed that a victorious Germany would inevitably dominate the continent. The British empire was in no immediate danger; Britain did not go to war in order to crush the German fleet, but to save France [352; 355]. The naval race had helped to embitter the British public against Germany, to turn their animosity away from the traditional enemies, France and Russia; and the German invasion of Belgium was instrumental in confirming the British in the righteousness of their cause. But the men making the decisions would have led Britain into war regardless of the invasion of Belgium [331; 351].

The First World War was not inevitable. Although it is essential to understand the underlying factors that formed the background to the July crisis, it is equally essential to see how the immediate circumstances of the crisis fit into this background in a particular, and perhaps unique, way [146]. Europe was not a powder-keg waiting to explode; one crisis did not lead necessarily to another in an escalating series of confrontations that made war more and more difficult to avoid. Europe had successfully weathered a number of storms in the recent past; the alliances were not rigidly fixed; the war plans were always being revised and need not necessarily have come into play. It is difficult to imagine a crisis in the far east, in north Africa or the Mediterranean that would have unleashed the series of events that arose from the assassination in Sarajevo [138]. The First World War was, in the final analysis, fought to determine who would control the future of the middle east; whoever won this struggle would, it was believed, be in a position to dominate all of Europe. Germany and her ally made the bid for control; Russia and her allies resolved to stop them [170; 193].

Most difficult to answer is the question of what part popular attitudes played in the coming of war. The organised working-class movements of pre-war Europe took the position that wars were caused by capitalist competition and that they were fought for the interests of the bourgeoisie – not for those whose lives would be lost or whose bodies would be ruined [95]. Some socialists stood up for their beliefs when war broke out, but they soon proved to represent only a small minority [350]. Organised pacifism had also been a popular phenomenon before 1914, particularly when the movement focused on disarmament or on international law as the means of preventing conflicts [311; 358]. Occasionally, these ideas even received official sanction [281]. But many pacifists abandoned their beliefs when war was declared. And the popularity of militarism proved to be too strong to overcome in 1914: decades of drilling, marching and flag-waving fused with popular nationalism and xenophobia to create a lethal combination. Whether we have learned from the experience of 1914, or whether we have forgotten its lessons, will be up to a new generation of students to decide.

PART FIVE: DOCUMENTS

DOCUMENT 1   **THE DUAL ALLIANCE**

This alliance between Germany and Austria was signed on 7 October 1879, and consisted of four articles. Articles III and IV provided for a five-year renewable term for the treaty and that the treaty should be kept secret, but the tsar was to be informed that an attack on either of the signatories would be regarded as an attack on both of them.

ART. I. Should, contrary to their hope, and against the loyal desire of the two High Contracting Parties, one of the two Empires be attacked by Russia, the High Contracting Parties are bound to come to the assistance one of the other with the whole war strength of their Empires, and accordingly only to conclude peace together and upon mutual agreement.

ART. II. Should one of the High Contracting Parties be attacked by another Power, the other High Contracting Party binds itself hereby, not only not to support the aggressor against its high Ally, but to observe at least a benevolent neutral attitude towards its fellow Contracting Party.

Should, however, the attacking party in such a case be supported by Russia, either by an active co-operation or by military measures which constitute a menace to the Party attacked, then the obligation stipulated in Article I of this Treaty, for reciprocal assistance with the whole fighting force, becomes equally operative, and the conduct of the war by the two High Contracting Parties shall in this case also be in common until the conclusion of a common peace.

Reprinted in *Key Treaties for the Great Powers 1814–1914, Vol. 2: 1871–1914*, ed. Michael Hurst, David and Charles, 1974, p. 590.

DOCUMENT 2   **THE TRIPLE ALLIANCE**

This treaty between Austria-Hungary, Germany and Italy was signed on 20 May 1882. Further articles provided for a term of five years and that the treaty should remain secret.

ART. I. The High Contracting Parties mutually promise peace and friendship, and will enter into no alliance or engagement directed against any one of their States.

They engage to proceed to an exchange of ideas on political and economic questions of a general nature which may arise, and they further promise one another mutual support within the limits of their own interests.

ART. II. In case Italy, without direct provocation on her part, should be attacked by France for any reason whatsoever, the two other Contracting Parties shall be bound to lend help and assistance with all their forces to the Party attacked.

This same obligation shall devolve upon Italy in case of any aggression without direct provocation by France against Germany.

ART III. If one, or two, of the High Contracting Parties, without direct provocation on their part, should chance to be attacked and to be engaged in a war with two or more Great Powers nonsignatory to the present Treaty, the *casus foederis* will arise simultaneously for all the High Contracting Parties.

ART. IV. In case a Great Power nonsignatory to the present Treaty should threaten the security of the states of one of the High Contracting Parties, and the threatened Party should find itself forced on that account to make war against it, the two others bind themselves to observe towards their Ally a benevolent neutrality. Each of them reserves to itself, in this case, the right to take part in the war, if it should see fit, to make common cause with its Ally.

ART. V. If the peace of any of the High Contracting Parties should chance to be threatened under the circumstances foreseen by the preceding Articles, the High Contracting Parties shall take counsel together in ample time as to the military measures to be taken with a view to eventual co-operation.

They engage henceforward, in all cases of common participation in a war, to conclude neither armistice, nor peace, nor treaty, except by common agreement among themselves.

Key Treaties, pp. 611–12.

DOCUMENT 3   BISMARCK'S EASTERN POLICY

After his resignation in 1890, Bismarck was anxious to clarify the difference between his conservative policy in the East, and the apparently adventurous one of Wilhelm II.

... in the future not only military equipment but also a correct political eye will be required to guide the German ship of state through the currents of coalitions to which we are exposed in consequence of our geographical position and our previous history. We shall not avoid the dangers which lie in the bosom of the future by amiability and commercial *pourboires* to friendly Powers. We should only increase the greed of our former friends and teach them to reckon on our anxieties and necessities . . . Our reputation and our security will develop all the more permanently, the more, in all conflicts which do not immediately touch us, we hold ourselves in reserve and do not show ourselves sensitive to every attempt to stir up and utilise our vanity . . . Germany would be guilty of a great folly if in Eastern struggles which did not affect her interests she were to take a side sooner than the other Powers who were more directly concerned . . . in future Eastern negotiations Germany, by holding back, will be able to turn to its advantage the fact that it is the Power which has least interest in Oriental questions . . .

If Germany has the advantage that her policy is free from direct interests in the East, on the other side is the disadvantage of the central and exposed position of the German Empire, with its extended frontier which has to be defended on every side, and the ease with which anti-German coalitions are made. At the same time Germany is perhaps the single Great Power in Europe which is not tempted by any objects which can only be attained by a successful war. It is our interest to maintain peace, while without exception our continental neighbours have wishes, either secret or officially avowed, which cannot be fulfilled except by war . . . we must do our best to prevent war or limit it.

Otto von Bismarck, *Bismarck: The Memoirs*, Vol. 2, Howard Fertig, 1966, pp. 290–2.

DOCUMENT 4   THE REINSURANCE TREATY

This treaty was signed between Germany and Russia on 18 June 1887 and was to remain in force for three years.

ART. I. In case one of the High Contracting Parties should find itself at war with a third great Power, the other would maintain a benevolent neutrality towards it, and would devote its efforts to the localization of the conflict. This provision would not apply to a war against Austria or France in case this war should result from an attack directed against one of these two latter Powers by one of the High Contracting Parties.
ART. II. Germany recognizes the rights historically acquired by Russia in the Balkan Peninsula, and particularly the legitimacy of her preponderant and decisive influence in Bulgaria and in Eastern Rumelia. The two Courts engage to admit no modification of the territorial *status quo* of the said peninsula without a previous agreement between them, and to oppose, as occasion arises, every attempt to disturb this *status quo* or to modify it without their consent.

ART. III. The two Courts recognize the European and mutually obligatory character of the principle of the closing of the Straits of the Bosphorus and of the Dardanelles, founded on international law, confirmed by treaties, and summed up in the declaration of the second Plenipotentiary of Russia at the session of July 12 of the Congress of Berlin (Protocol 19).

They will take care in common that Turkey shall make no exception to this rule in favour of the interests of any Government whatsoever, by lending to warlike operations of a belligerent power the portion of its Empire constituted by the Straits. In case of infringement, or to prevent it if such infringement should be in prospect, the two Courts will inform Turkey that they would regard her, in that event, as putting herself in a state of war towards the injured Party, and as depriving herself thenceforth of the benefits of the security assured to her territorial *status quo* by the Treaty of Berlin.

Key Treaties, p. 646.

DOCUMENT 5   THE 'WILLY-NICKY' CORRESPONDENCE

Wilhelm II hoped, by means of a friendly personal correspondence with Nicholas II (which was conducted in English), to deflect Russia's ambitions from Europe to Asia, and to arouse the tsar's fears of too close a relationship with revolutionary France.

26 April 1895 . . . I shall certainly do all in my power to keep Europe quiet, and also guard the rear of Russia so that nobody shall hamper your action towards the Far East!

For that is clearly the great task of the future for Russia to cultivate the Asian Continent and to defend Europe from the inroads of the Great Yellow race. In this you will always find me on your side, ready to help you as best I can . . .

26 September 1895 . . . The proposed new Corps would increase the already overwhelming French forces to 5 Corps, and constitutes a threat as well as a serious danger to my country . . . [it] has made people uneasy here and given affairs an ugly look, as if Russia would like France to be offensive against Germany with the hopes of help from the first named . . . I perfectly know that you personally do not dream of attacking us, but still you cannot be astonished that the European Powers get alarmed seeing how the presence of your officers and high officials in official way in France fans the inflamable [sic] Frenchman into a white heated passion and strengthens the cause of Chauvinism and Revanche! . . . if France goes on openly or secretly encouraged like this to violate all rules of international courtesy and Peace in peace times, one fine day my dearest Nicky you will find yourself *nolens volens* suddenly embroiled in the most horrible of wars Europe ever saw! . . .

25 October 1895 . . . it is not a *fact* of the *Rapport* or friendship between Russia and France that makes one uneasy . . . but the danger which is brought to our Principle of Monarchism through the lifting up [of] the Republic on a pedestal by the form under which the friendship is shown. The constant appearance of Princes, Grand-dukes, statesmen, Generals in 'full fig' at reviews, burials, dinners, races, with the head of the Republic or in his entourage makes Republicains [sic] . . . believe that they are quite honest excellent people with whom Princes can consort and feel at home! . . . Dont forget that Jaurès . . . sits on the throne of the King and Queen of France 'by the Grace of God' whose heads Frenchmen Republicans cut off. The Blood of their Majesties is still on that country! Look at it, has it since then ever been happy or quiet again? Has it not staggered from bloodshed to bloodshed? And in its great moments did it not go from war to war? Till it soused all Europe and Russia in streams of blood? Till at last it had the Commune over again? Nicky take my word on it the curse of God has stricken that people forever!

If unfortunately, as a result of a mature examination of the situation, Germany and Italy should both recognize that the maintenance of the *status quo* has become impossible, Germany engages, after a formal and previous agreement, to support Italy in any action in the form of occupation or other taking of guaranty which the latter should undertake in these same regions with a view to an interest of equilibrium and of legitimate compensation.

It is understood that in such an eventuality the two Powers would seek to place themselves likewise in agreement with England.

Kaiser Wilhelm II, [30], pp. 10–11, 20–1, 23–5.

DOCUMENT 6   THE FRANCO-RUSSIAN ALLIANCE

The alliance between France and Russia was created in an exchange of letters between their foreign ministers in August 1891; the alliance was not formally ratified until the following year.

Letter of M. de Giers, Minister of Foreign Affairs of Russia, to M. de Mohrenheim, Ambassador of Russia at Paris. Petersburg, August 9/21, 1891.

The situation created in Europe by the open renewal of the Triple Alliance and the more or less probable adhesion of Great Britain to the political aims which that alliance pursues, has, during the recent sojourn here of M. de Laboulaye, prompted an exchange of ideas between the former Ambassador of France and myself, tending to define the attitude which, as things now stand and in the presence of certain eventualities, might best suit our respective Governments, which, having kept out of any league, are none the less sincerely desirous of surrounding the maintenance of peace with the most efficacious guarantees.

It is thus that we have been led to formulate the two points below:

1. In order to define and consecrate the cordial understanding which unites them, and desirous of contributing in common agreement to the maintenance of the peace which forms the object of their sincerest aspirations, the two Governments declare that they will take counsel together upon every question of a nature to jeopardize the general peace;

2. In case that peace should be actually in danger, and especially if one of the two parties should be threatened with an aggression, the two parties undertake to reach an understanding on the measures whose immediate and simultaneous adoption would be imposed upon the two Governments by the realization of this eventuality . . .

Key Treaties, p. 663.

DOCUMENT 7   FRANCO-RUSSIAN MILITARY
             CONVENTION

The military co-operation provided for in Document 9 was outlined in this 1892 draft agreement, which was approved in December 1893.

France and Russia, being animated by an equal desire to preserve peace, and having no other object than to meet the necessities of a defensive war, provoked by an attack of the forces of the Triple Alliance against the one or the other of them, have agreed upon the following provisions:

1. If France is attacked by Germany, or by Italy supported by Germany, Russia shall employ all her available forces to attack Germany.

If Russia is attacked by Germany, or by Austria supported by Germany, France shall employ all her available forces to fight Germany.

2. In case the forces of the Triple Alliance, or of one of the Powers composing it, should mobilize, France and Russia, at the first news of the event and without the necessity of any previous concert, shall mobilize immediately and simultaneously the whole of their forces and shall move them as close as possible to their frontiers.

3. The available forces to be employed against Germany shall be, on the part of France, 1,300,000 men, on the part of Russia, 700,000 or 800,000 men.

These forces shall engage to the full, with all speed, in order that Germany may have to fight at the same time on the East and on the West.

4. The General Staffs of the Armies of the two countries shall co-operate with each other at all times in the preparation and facilitation of the execution of the measures above foreseen.

They shall communicate to each other, while there is still peace, all information relative to the armies of the Triple Alliance which is or shall be within their knowledge.

Ways and means of corresponding in times of war shall be studied and arranged in advance.

5. France and Russia shall not conclude peace separately.

6. The present Convention shall have the same duration as the Triple Alliance.

7. All the clauses above enumerated shall be kept rigorously secret.

Key Treaties, pp. 668–9.

DOCUMENT 8   GERMANY AND 'WORLD POLICIES'

The German Chancellor, Prince Bernhard von Bülow, explained in a speech to the Reichstag on 11 December 1899 why the deputies must support a large army and navy.

... recent decades have brought to Germany great good fortune and power and prosperity. Good fortune and growing prosperity in one quarter are not always greeted in others with pure satisfaction; they may awaken envy. Envy plays a great part in the life of individuals and in the life of nations. There is a great deal of envy of us in the world, political envy and economic envy ... [the] times of political impotence and economic and political insignificance must not return. We do not intend again to be ... the bondmen of humanity. The one condition, however, on which alone we shall maintain our position is that we realize that without power, without a strong army and a strong navy, there can be no welfare for us. The means of fighting the battle for existence in this world without strong armaments on land and water, for a nation soon to count sixty millions, living in the centre of Europe and at the same time stretching out its economic feelers in all directions, have not yet been found. In the coming century the German nation will be either the hammer or the anvil.

Prince von Bülow, [16], p. 353.

DOCUMENT 9   THE ANGLO-JAPANESE ALLIANCE

This agreement was made on 30 January 1902; further articles provided for consultation in case the interests of either signatory were jeopardised, and for a renewable term of five years.

ART. I. The High Contracting Parties, having mutually recognized the independence of China and Korea, declare themselves to be entirely uninfluenced by any aggressive tendencies in either country. Having in view, however, their special interests of which those of Great Britain relate principally to China, while Japan, in addition to the interests which she possesses in China, is interested in a peculiar degree politically as well as commercially and industrially in Korea, the High Contracting Parties recognize that it will be admissible for either of them to take such measures as may be indispensable in order to safeguard those interests if threatened either by the aggressive action of any other Power, or by disturbances arising in China or Korea, and necessitating the intervention of either of the High Contracting Parties for the protection of the lives and property of its subjects.

ART. II. If either Great Britain or Japan, in the defence of their respective interests as above described, should become involved in war with another Power, the other High Contracting Party will maintain a strict neutrality, and use its efforts to prevent other Powers from joining in hostilities against its ally.

ART. III. If, in the above event, any other Power or Powers should join in hostilities against that ally, the other High Contracting Party will come to its assistance, and will conduct the war in common, and make peace in mutual agreement with it.

Key Treaties, pp. 726–7.

DOCUMENT 10   RUSSIA'S BALKAN POLICY

Although the memoirs and autobiographies of the leading participants in the events of 1914 are invariably self-serving, they are still useful and interesting. Here the Russian foreign minister, Serge Sazonov, explains both the idealistic and the practical components of Russian policy.

. . . Russia's historical mission – the emancipation of the Christian peoples of the Balkan peninsula from the Turkish yoke – was almost fulfilled by the beginning of the twentieth century; its completion could be left to the efforts of the liberated peoples themselves . . . Although these younger countries no longer needed the guardianship of Russia, they were not yet strong enough to dispense with her help in the event of any attempt upon their national existence by warlike Teutonism. Serbia in particular was exposed to this danger, having become the object of the decorously concealed covetousness of Austrian diplomacy . . . [Russia's] sole and unchanging object was to see that those Balkan peoples who had been freed by her age-long efforts and sacrifices should not fall under the influence of Powers hostile to her, or become the obedient tools of their political intrigues. The ultimate aim of Russian policy was to obtain free access to the Mediterranean, and to be in a position to defend her Black Sea coasts against the constant threat of the irruption of hostile naval forces through the Bosphorus . . .

Russia proclaimed and defended the principle of the independence of the Balkan States as fundamentally just, in view of their inalienable right to an independent political existence. In our eyes this principle, in addition to its moral significance, had also a practical value; for not only was it not detrimental to any of Russia's vital interests, but it indirectly furthered their maintenance. 'The Balkan Peninsula for the Balkan peoples' was the formula which comprised the aspirations and aims of Russian policy; it precluded the possibility of the political predominance, and still more of the sovereignty in the Balkans, of a foreign Power hostile to Balkan Slavdom and to Russia.

S. Sazonov, [54], pp. 49–51.

DOCUMENT 11   THE KAISER'S 'BLANK CHEQUE' TO AUSTRIA

This is the report of the famous conversation between Wilhelm II and the Austrian ambassador in Berlin, Count von Szögyény-Marich, in which the kaiser seemed to promise his support for Austria under any conditions.

Count Szögyény to Count Berchtold (Austro-Hungarian Foreign Minister)

Berlin 5 July 1914   tel.237 Strictly Confidential
. . . the Kaiser authorised me to inform our gracious majesty that we might in this case, as in all others, rely upon Germany's full support . . . he did not doubt in the least that Herr von Bethmann Hollweg would agree with him. Especially as far as our action against Serbia was concerned. But it was his (Kaiser Wilhelm's) opinion that this action must not be delayed. Russia's attitude will no doubt be hostile, but for this he had for years prepared, and should a war between Austria-Hungary and Russia be unavoidable, we might be convinced that Germany, our old faithful ally, would stand at our side. Russia at the present time was in no way prepared for war, and would think twice before it appealed to arms . . . if we had really recognised the necessity of warlike action against Serbia, he (Kaiser Wilhelm) would regret if we did not make use of the present moment, which is all in our favour . . .

Quoted in Geiss, [7], p. 77.

DOCUMENT 12   GERMANY'S BALKAN POLICY

Gotlieb von Jagow, the German secretary for foreign affairs, explained to his ambassador in London, Prince Karl Lichnowsky, the reasons for Germany's policy in the July crisis. Lichnowsky had been critical of Germany's policy of supporting Austria-Hungary.

18 July 1914

Austria no longer intends to tolerate the sapping activities of the Serbians, and just as little does she intend to tolerate longer the continuously provocative attitude of her small neighbour at Belgrade . . . She fully realises that she has neglected many opportunities, and that she is still able to act, though in a few years she may no longer be able to do so. Austria is now going to force a showdown with Serbia, and has told us so. During the whole Balkan crisis we mediated successfully in the interest of peace, without forcing Austria to passivity at any of the critical moments. The fact that notwithstanding that we have often, with injustice, been accused of trimming and shuffling, makes no difference to me. Nor have we at the present time forced Austria to her decision. But we neither could nor should attempt to stay her hand. If we should do that, Austria would have the right to reproach us (and we ourselves) with having deprived her of her last chance of political rehabilitation. And then the process of her wasting away and of her internal decay would be still further accelerated. Her standing in the Balkans would be gone forever. You will undoubtedly agree with me that the absolute establishment of the Russian hegemony in the Balkans is, indirectly, not permissible, even for us. The maintenance of Austria, and, in fact, of the most powerful Austria possible, is a necessity for us both for internal and external reasons. That she cannot be maintained forever, I will willingly admit. But in the meantime we may perhaps be able to arrange other combinations.

We must attempt to localise the conflict between Austria and Serbia. Whether we shall succeed in this will depend first on Russia, and secondly on the moderating influence of Russia's allies. The more determined Austria shows herself, the more energetically we support her, so much the more quiet will Russia remain. To be sure, there will be some agitation in St Petersburg, but, on the whole, Russia is not ready to strike at present. Nor will France or England be anxious for war at the present time. According to all competent observation, Russia will be prepared to fight in a few years. Then she will crush us by the number of her soldiers; then she will have built her Baltic Sea fleet and her strategic railroads. Our group, in the meantime, will have become weaker right along.

Quoted in Geiss, [7], pp. 122–3.

DOCUMENT 13   RUSSIA AND THE THREAT OF
REVOLUTION

*Although some Russians feared that war would result in revolution, most of
those in government, as this recollection by Nicolas de Basily (of the
ministry of foreign affairs) of a conversation with Hohenloe (the Austrian
military attaché in St Petersburg) shows, felt confident or preferred to take
the risk rather than accept humiliation.*

One evening in July 1914 . . . [Hohenloe and I] took the road out of St.
Petersburg toward Finland. The huge forests of black pine were immersed in
absolute silence, undisturbed by the slightest breath of air. It was the time
of the marvelous white nights of the northern summer. The sun had scarcely
disappeared beneath the horizon only to rise again about an hour later. A
faint, pale light illuminated the landscape, sad and austere, and increased in
us a certain state of anxiety inspired by the recent political news . . .

[We] could not turn our thoughts from the tension growing day by day
between our two countries. We could already foresee some of the possible
consequences of the Sarajevo murder. Taking me by the arm, Hohenloe
said, 'Do you understand that you cannot go to war? If you do, you will
expose yourself to revolution and to the ruin of your power.' I replied to
my friend that while some changes within Russia and perhaps even a
serious internal crisis were probable in the future, at present there was no
indication of internal trouble. Public opinion was clamoring for an
intervention in support of Serbia, and the Russian government would have
the approval of the entire nation if it judged itself obliged to act. I added
forcefully, 'You commit a serious error of calculation in supposing that fear
of a revolution will prevent Russia from fulfilling its national duty now. As
for the future, who can predict that with certainty?'

N. de Basily, [13], pp. 89–90.

DOCUMENT 14   THE POLICY OF SIR EDWARD GREY

*In the 1920s Sir Edward Grey tried to defend himself against charges that
he had contributed to the outbreak of war by following a weak and
vacillating policy at the time of the July crisis.*

Certain things stand out very clearly in my memory of the week before the
war. The general suffering and the private griefs of the war have left scars
in the memory of all who experienced them; but the week before the war
also left marks on those who had responsibility – marks indelible, too deep
to be obscured even by the distress of what followed.

What was said or done by me will be most clearly explained and best understood by stating the considerations and convictions that were dominant in my mind throughout that week . . .

1. A conviction that a great European war under modern conditions would be a catastrophe for which previous wars afforded no precedent . . . I thought this must be obvious to everyone else, as it seemed obvious to me; and that, if once it became apparent that we were on the edge, all the Great Powers would call a halt and recoil from the abyss.

2. That Germany was so immensely strong and Austria so dependent upon German strength that the word and will of Germany would at the critical moment be decisive with Austria. It was therefore to Germany that we must address ourselves.

3. That, if war came, the interest of Britain required that we should not stand aside, while France fought alone in the West, but must support her. I knew it to be very doubtful whether the Cabinet, Parliament and the country would take this view on the outbreak of war, and through the whole of this week I had in view the probable contingency that we should not decide at the critical moment to support France. In that event I should have to resign . . .

4. A clear view that no pledge must be given, no hope even held out to France and Russia, which it was doubtful whether this country would fulfil. One danger I saw so hideous that it must be avoided and guarded against at every word. It was that France and Russia might face the ordeal of war with Germany relying upon our support; that this support might not be forthcoming, and that we might then, when it was too late, be held responsible by them for having let them in for a disastrous war . . .

The notion of being involved in war about a Balkan quarrel was repugnant . . . there was no sentiment urging us to go into a war on Serbia's behalf. If France were involved, it would not be in any quarrel in which we owed her good-will . . . It would indeed not be in any quarrel of her own at all; it would be because she, as Russia's Ally, had the misfortune to be involved in a Russian quarrel . . . What, it was asked, was the good of keeping so carefully clear of alliances and obligations if we were to be drawn into European war in such a quarrel as this? . . . Some of us felt that the considerations stated above did not touch the true issue. We felt that to stand aside would mean the domination of Germany; the subordination of France and Russia; the isolation of Britain, the hatred of her by both those who had feared and those who had wished for her intervention in the war; and ultimately that Germany would wield the whole power of the Continent. How would she use it as regards Britain? Could anyone feel comfortable about that question? Could anyone give to it truthfully in his heart any but a sinister and foreboding answer?

Viscount Grey, [31], Vol. 1, pp. 311–3, 335, 337.

DOCUMENT 15   THE AUSTRIAN ULTIMATUM

*The preamble to the following ultimatum asserted that the Serbian
government was culpable in the assassination because it had tolerated the
rise of a subversive movement within its territory and had done nothing to
prevent its criminal activities.*

... the Royal Government finds itself obliged to demand from the Serbian
Government an official assurance that it condemns the propaganda directed
against Austria-Hungary and in their entirety the dealings whose ultimate
aim it is to disjoin parts of the territory belonging to the Monarchy and that
it pledges itself to suppress with all the means in its power this criminal and
terrorist propaganda.

With a view to giving these assurances a solemn character, the Royal
Serbian Government will publish the following declaration on the first page
of its official press-organ of 26/13 July:

'The Royal Serbian Government condemns the propaganda directed
against Austria-Hungary, that is the entirety of the ambitions, whose
ultimate aim it is to disjoin parts of the territory belonging to the Austrian-
Hungarian Monarchy and regrets sincerely the horrible consequences of
these criminal ambitions.

The Royal Serbian Government regrets that Serbian officers and officials
have taken part in the propaganda above-mentioned and thereby imperilled
the friendly and neighbourly relations, which the Royal Government had
solemnly promised to cultivate in its declaration of 31 March 1909.

The Royal Government, which condemns and rejects every thought and
every attempt to interfere in behalf of the inhabitants of any part of
Austria-Hungary, considers it a duty to warn officers, officials and indeed
all the inhabitants of the kingdom, that it will in future use great severity
against such persons, as will be found guilty of similar doings, which the
Government will make every effort to suppress.'

This declaration will at the same time be communicated to the Royal
army by an order of His Majesty the King, and will besides be published in
the official organ of the army.

The Royal Serbian Government will overmore pledge itself to the
following:

1. To suppress every publication likely to inspire hatred and contempt
against the Monarchy or whose general tendencies are directed against the
integrity of the latter;
2. to begin immediately dissolving the society called *Narodna odbrana*; to
seize all its means of propaganda and to act in the same way against all the
societies and associations in Serbia, which are busy with the propaganda
against Austria-Hungary; the Royal Government will take the necessary

measures to prevent these societies continuing their efforts under another name or in another form;

3. to eliminate without delay from public instruction everything that serves or might serve the propaganda against Austria-Hungary, both where teachers or books are concerned;

4. to remove from military service and from the administration all officers and officials who are guilty of having taken part in the propaganda against Austria-Hungary, whose names and the proofs of whose guilt the Imp. and Royal Government will communicate to the Royal Government;

5. to consent that Imp. and Royal Officials assist in Serbia in the suppressing of the subversive movement directed against the territorial integrity of the Monarchy;

6. to have a judicial enquiry instituted against all those who took part in the plot of 28 June, if they are to be found on Serbian territory; the Imp. and Royal Government will delegate organs who will take an active part in these enquiries;

7. to arrest without delay Major Voija Tankosic and a certain Milan Ciganovic, a Serbian government official, both compromised by the results of the enquiry;

8. to take effective measures so as to prevent the Serbian authorities from taking part in the smuggling of weapons and explosives across the frontier; to dismiss from service and severely punish those organs of the frontier service at Schabatz and Loznica, who helped the perpetrators of the crime of Sarajevo to reach Bosnia in safety;

9. to give the Imp. and Royal Government an explanation of the unjustified remarks of high Serbian functionaries in Serbia as well as in foreign countries, who, notwithstanding their official positions, did not hesitate to speak in hostile terms of Austria-Hungary in interviews given just after the event of 28 June;

10. to inform the Imp. and Royal Government without delay that the measures summed up in the above points have been carried out.

Quoted in Geiss, [7], pp. 144–5.

DOCUMENT 16   THE RUSSIAN MOBILISATION

The French ambassador in St Petersburg, Maurice Paléologue, recorded Russia's explanation of her decision to commence a general mobilisation.

29 July
At eleven o'clock tonight, Nicholas-Alexandrovitch Basily, Deputy-Director of the chancellery of the Foreign Office, appeared at my embassy. He came to tell me that the imperious language used by the German Ambassador this afternoon has decided the Russian Government (1) to order this very night

the mobilization of the thirteen corps earmarked for operations against Austria-Hungary; (2) secretly to commence general mobilization.

These last words made me jump:

'Isn't it possible for them to confine themselves – provisionally at any rate – to a partial mobilization?'

'No. The question has just been gone into thoroughly by a council of our highest military officers. They have come to the conclusion that in existing circumstances the Russian Government has no choice between partial and general mobilization as from the technical point of view a partial mobilization could be carried out only at the price of dislocating the entire machinery of general mobilization. So if to-day we stopped at mobilizing the thirteen corps destined for operations against Austria and tomorrow Germany decided to give her ally military support, we should be powerless to defend ourselves on the frontiers of Poland and East Prussia.'

M. Paléologue, [43], p. 32.

CHRONOLOGY OF EVENTS

1871   10 May, Treaty of Frankfurt: end of Franco-Prussian war
1872   First *Dreikaiserbund*
1875   'Is War in Sight?' crisis
1878   Russo-Turkish War; Great Eastern Crisis
1879   7 October, Dual Alliance signed by Germany and Austria-Hungary
1881   Second *Dreikaiserbund*
1882   20 May, Italy joins Germany and Austria-Hungary in Triple Alliance
1886   Penjdeh Crisis
1887   February–March, first Mediterranean agreement
1887   18 June, Russo-German Reinsurance Treaty signed
1887   December, second Mediterranean agreement
1888   15 June, Wilhelm II becomes emperor
1890   15 March, Bismarck dismissed
1890   18 June, Reinsurance Treaty not renewed
1891   27 August, Franco-Russian political agreement
1892   17 August, Franco-Russian military convention drafted
1893   17 January, Franco-Russian military convention ratified
1894   4 January, Franco-Russian alliance signed
1897   27 April, Russia and Austria-Hungary agree to put Balkans 'on ice'
1898   First German Naval Law
1899   War in South Africa ('Boer War') begins
1900   Second German Naval Law
1900   Anglo-German agreement on China
1900   December, Secret agreement signed between Italy and France
1902   War in South Africa ('Boer War') ends
1902   30 January, Anglo-Japanese alliance signed
1903   2 October, Russia and Austria-Hungary conclude the Murzsteg agreement
1904   8 February, Japan attacks Russia

1904   8 April, Anglo-French entente
1904   Russo-German Commercial Agreement
1905   22 January, 'Bloody Sunday' in St Petersburg
1905   January, French military mission arrives at Fez, Morocco
1905   31 March, Kaiser Wilhelm II lands at Tangier, Morocco
1905   27 May, Battle of Tsushima
1905   24 July, Treaty of Björkö
1905   12 August, the Anglo-Japanese alliance revised
1905   5 September, Treaty of Portsmouth ends Russo-Japanese War
1905   30 October, the October Manifesto signed by Tsar Nicholas II
1906   16 January, Algeciras Conference begins
1906   7 April, Algeciras Act signed
1906   17 April, France lends 2,250,000,000 francs to Russia
1906   6 May, the 'Fundamental Laws' in Russia establish a constitution and create the Duma
1906   5 June, Third Naval Law in Germany ratified by Reichstag
1907   31 August, Anglo-Russian entente
1908   16 September, Büchlau agreement between Izvolsky and Aehrenthal
1908   6 October, Bosnia and Herzegovina annexed by Austria-Hungary
1909   February, Russia recognises the Austro-Hungarian annexation of Bosnia and Herzegovina
1909   8 February, Franco-German agreement on Morocco
1911   21 May, French troops occupy Fez, Morocco
1911   1 July, German gunboat, *Panther*, arrives in Agadir
1911   21 July, Lloyd George's speech on Morocco at the Mansion House
1911   4 November, Franco-German agreement on Morocco
1912   February, Lord Haldane undertakes mission to Germany
1912   13 March, alliance signed between Serbia and Bulgaria
1912   29 May, Greece joins Serbia and Bulgaria in 'Balkan League'
1912   September, Italy invades Libya
1912   18 October, First Balkan War begins
1912   December, Conference of Ambassadors meets in London to settle First Balkan War
1913   31 May, Treaty of London ends First Balkan War
1913   29 June, Second Balkan War begins
1913   11 August, Treaty of Bucharest ends Second Balkan War
1913   30 September, Treaty of Constantinople signed

1913	November, Russia launches the 'Great Military Programme'
1914	28 June, Archduke Franz Ferdinand assassinated at Sarajevo
1914	23 July, Austria issues ultimatum to Serbia
1914	28 July, Austria declares war on Serbia
1914	28 July, Russia orders 'partial' mobilisation
1914	30 July, Russia orders general mobilisation for following day
1914	30 July, Austria orders general mobilisation for following day
1914	31 July, German ultimatum to Russia
1914	1 August, Germany declares war on Russia
1914	3 August, Germany declares war on France
1914	4 August, German troops cross Belgian frontier
1914	4 August, Britain declares war on Germany

GUIDE TO CHARACTERS

Aehrenthal, Count Alois von (1854–1912). Austrian diplomat and statesman; ambassador in St Petersburg, 1899–1906; Austro-Hungarian minister of foreign affairs, 1906–12.

Alexander I (1777–1825). Son of Paul I; tsar of Russia, 1801–25.

Alexeiev, Evgeny Ivanovich (1843–1920). Russian admiral, illegitimate son of Alexander II, uncle of Nicholas II; appointed Viceroy of the Far East in 1903.

Barrère, Camille (1851–1940). French diplomat; ambassador to Italy, 1897–1924.

Berchtold, Count Leopold von (1863–1942). Austrian diplomat and statesman; ambassador in Paris, 1894–99; in London, 1899–1906; in St Petersburg, 1906–12; Austro-Hungarian minister of foreign affairs, 1912–15.

Bertie, Francis (1st Viscount Bertie of Thame) (1844–1919). British diplomat; assistant under-secretary of state for foreign affairs, 1894–1903; ambassador in Rome, 1903–05; ambassador in Paris, 1905–18.

Bethmann Hollweg, Theobald von (1856–1921). Prussian minister of the interior, 1905–07; German minister of the interior, 1907–09; German chancellor, 1909–17.

Bezobrazov, Alexander Mikhailovich (1866–1933). Russian statesman; state secretary and member of Special Committee for the Affairs of the Far East, 1903–05.

Bismarck, Prince Otto von (1815–98). German statesman; elected to Prussian parliament in 1848; Prussian member of federal Diet at Frankfurt, 1851–59; ambassador to Russia and France, 1859–62; minister-president of Prussia, 1862–71; chancellor of North German Confederation, 1866–71; chancellor of Germany, 1871–90.

Boulanger, General Georges (1837–91). French soldier and statesman; minister of war, 1886–87; his appointment of republicans to military posts in place of royalists led to his dismissal, a political crisis and then his exile.

Bülow, Bernhard von (1849–1929). German statesman; foreign minister, 1897–1900; chancellor, 1900–09.

Burns, John (1858–1943). British statesman; elected to House of Commons, 1892; president of local government board, 1905–14; president of the board of trade, 1914; resigned during July crisis.

Cambon, Paul (1843–1924). French diplomat; ambassador to Britain, 1898–1921.

Conrad von Hötzendorf, Count (1852–1925). Austrian soldier; chief of Austro-Hungarian general staff, 1906–11, 1912–17.

Cromer, 1st Earl of (Evelyn Baring, 1841–1917). British colonial administrator; British agent and consul-general in Egypt, 1883–1907.

Crowe, Sir Eyre (1864–1925). British administrator; assistant under-secretary of state for foreign affairs, 1912–20.

Cruppi, Jean (1855–1933). French statesman; minister of foreign affairs, 1911; minister of justice, 1911–12.

Delcassé, Théophile (1852–1923). French statesman; elected deputy, 1889; minister of colonies, 1893–95; foreign minister, 1898–1905; naval minister, 1911–13; foreign minister, 1914–15.

Edward VII (1841–1910). Son of Queen Victoria; succeeded her as king of Great Britain and Ireland and emperor of India in 1901.

Franz Joseph (1830–1916). Emperor of Austria, 1848–1916; king of Hungary, 1867–1916.

Franz Ferdinand, Archduke (1863–1914). Nephew of the Emperor Franz Joseph and, from 1896, heir to the throne of Austria-Hungary.

Garibaldi, Giuseppe (1807–82). Italian nationalist and hero of the *Risorgimento*; in 1860 he led an invasion of Sicily and later captured Naples, leading to their inclusion in the newly unified Italian state.

Lloyd George, David (1863–1945). British statesman; elected to the British parliament, 1890; entered the cabinet, 1905; chancellor of the exchequer, 1908–15; prime minister, 1916–22.

Grey, 1st Viscount (Sir Edward Grey) (1862–1933). Elected to British parliament, 1885; foreign secretary, 1905–16.

Haldane, Richard Burdon (1st Viscount Haldane) (1856–1928). Elected to British parliament, 1885; secretary of war, 1905–1912; lord chancellor, 1912–15 and 1924.

Hardinge, Charles (1st Baron Hardinge of Penshurst) (1858–1944). British diplomat and administrator; ambassador in St Petersburg, 1904–06; under-secretary of state for foreign affairs, 1906–10; viceroy of India, 1910–16.

Hobson, John Atkinson (1858–1940). English journalist and economist; author of *The War in South Africa* (1900), *The Psychology of Jingoism* (1901), *Imperialism: A Study* (1902), and *The Science of Wealth* (1911).

Holstein, Friedrich von (1837–1909). German administrator; served in foreign ministry, 1876–1906; although his highest post was as Director of the Political Section, he was very influential in the period 1890–1906.

Izvolsky, Alexander (1856–1919). Russian diplomat and statesman entered Russian diplomatic service, 1875; foreign minister, 1905–10; ambassador to France, 1910–16.

Joffre, Joseph Jacques Césaire (1852–1931). French soldier and administrator; vice-president of the higher war council, 1911–14; commander-in-chief, 1914–16.

Kiderlen-Wächter, Alfred von (1852–1912). German administrator; state secretary in the foreign office, 1910–13.

Lambsdorff, Count V.N. (1844–1907). Russian statesman; foreign minister, 1900–06.

Lansdowne, 5th Marquis of (Henry Charles Keith Petty-Fitzmaurice, 1845–1927). British statesman and administrator; secretary of war, 1895–1900; foreign secretary, 1900–05.

Liman von Sanders, Otto (1855–1929). German soldier; led German military commission to Constantinople, 1913; appointed inspector-general of Turkish army, 1914.

Loubet, Émile (1838–1929). French statesman; president, 1899–1906.

Metternich, Prince Klemens von (1773–1859). Austrian diplomat and statesman; ambassador during the Napoleonic Wars; minister of foreign affairs, 1809–48; chancellor, 1812–48.

Moltke, Helmuth ('the younger') (1848–1916). German soldier; chief of the Prussian general staff, 1906–14.

Napoleon I (Napoleon Bonaparte) (1769–1821). First Consul of France, 1799–1804; emperor, 1804–14.

Napoleon III (Charles Louis Napoleon Bonaparte) (1808–73). Son of Napoleon Bonaparte's brother Louis; elected president of the Second Republic, 1848; emperor, 1848–71; exiled, 1871–73.

Nicholas I (1796–1855). Son of Paul I; succeeded his brother, Alexander I, as tsar of Russia, 1825.

Nicholas II (1869–1918). Son of Alexander III of Russia; became tsar 1894; abdicated 1917; shot by revolutionaries, 1918.

Nicholas Nikolayevich, Grand-Duke (1856–1929). Russian soldier and administrator; nephew of Tsar Alexander II; commander-in-chief, 1914–17.

Nicolson, Sir Arthur (1849–1928). British diplomat and administrator; minister in Tangier, 1901–04; in Madrid, 1904–06; in St Petersburg, 1906–10; under-secretary of state for foreign affairs, 1910–16.

Poincaré, Raymond (1860–1934). French statesman; elected deputy, 1887; minister of education, 1893–94; minister of finance, 1894–95, 1906; senator, 1906–13; prime minister, 1912–13; president, 1913–20.

Prinetti, Giulio (1851–1908). Italian statesman; minister of foreign affairs, 1901–03.

Rouvier, Maurice (1842–1911). French statesman; elected deputy, 1871; minister of foreign affairs, 1902–05; prime minister, 1905–06, 1906–11.

Sazonov, Serge Dmitrievich (1861–1927). Russian statesman; minister of foreign affairs, 1910–16.

Schlieffen, Count Alfred von (1833–1913). German field-marshal and chief of the Prussian general staff, 1891–1906; designer of the Schlieffen plan, the basis of pre-war German military strategy.

Tirpitz, Alfred von (1849–1930). German admiral; secretary of state for the navy, 1897–1916; strategist responsible for the creation of the 'risk fleet' which began construction in 1898.

Tisza, István (1861–1918). Hungarian statesman; prime minister of Hungary, 1904–05, 1913–17; murdered, 1918.

Wilhelm II (1859–1941). Son of Emperor Frederick III; emperor of Germany and king of Prussia, 1888–1918; abdicated, 1918; exiled to Holland.

Witte, Serge (1849–1915). Russian statesman; minister of finance, 1892–1903; prime minister, 1905.

GLOSSARY

Anarchism A socio-political movement that rejects the coercive authority of the state in favour of individual freedom. Based on the ideas of two Russians, Mikhail Bakunin and Prince Peter Kropotkin, anarchism reached the height of its popularity in the decades before the First World War, when it came to be associated with violence and terrorism.

Ausgleich Literally, 'compromise', this constitutional re-arrangement within the Habsburg monarchy was instituted in 1867. It allowed for separate parliaments (*Diets*) and prime ministers in Austria and Hungary; the empire remained connected by means of a common emperor/king, a common army and navy and a customs unit.

Autocracy A loosely defined political term usually referring to absolute or despotic rule by an individual. Most often used in referring to the tsar, 'the autocrat of all the Russias'.

Boxers Term used to describe those Chinese who violently opposed foreign influence in China, 1899–1900. The name comes from their ritualised exercises known as 'harmony fists'. They attacked Christian missionaries, destroyed European property and besieged foreign legations in Peking for two months in June–August 1900.

Comité de l'Afrique Française A political association formed to promote French colonialism in Africa. It was a highly influential group and one of its presidents, Charles Jonnart, became French foreign minister in 1912.

Committee of Imperial Defence Established by the British government at the end of the South African War in an effort to improve strategic planning and overcome the traditional rivalry between the army and the navy. It proved largely ineffective in accomplishing its goals, although sub-committees did do some useful work.

Dreadnought A new class of battleship launched in Britain in 1906. Replacing coal with oil as fuel made these ships faster than previous models, and ten twelve-inch guns rather than four made them more powerful (and much more expensive). Earlier battleships were rendered obsolete and the Anglo-German naval race was intensified.

Dreikaiserbund Literally, the 'three emperors' league'. In the first league, formed by Germany, Russia and Austria-Hungary in 1873, the three agreed to consult with one another on matters of common concern. It was replaced by a more formal agreement in 1881 when each promised to remain neutral if one of the three fought a fourth.

Dual Monarchy The name used to refer to the Habsburg empire following the *Ausgleich* of 1867. It represented an agreement between the dominant Germans of Austria and the powerful Magyars of Hungary.

Duma The Russian parliament established after the revolution of 1905. Although this represented a significant concession on the part of the Russian monarchy, it was a weak and unrepresentative institution. Its powers were strictly limited, especially in the areas of defence, foreign policy and finance.

German Confederation An association (or *Bund*) of thirty-nine states in central Europe formed at the end of the Napoleonic Wars in 1815. Dominated by Austria, their representatives met in a *Diet* in Frankfurt, but this had very little authority. It collapsed when Prussia defeated Austria in 1866.

Holy Alliance Following the Napoleonic Wars, Tsar Alexander I drew up a document proclaiming that European rulers must henceforth be guided by Christian principles; most European states eventually adhered to it. But the phrase is usually used as a short-hand reference to the reactionary policies of Russia, Austria and Prussia.

Italia irredenta Literally, 'unredeemed Italy'. A popular movement in Italy following the wars of unification to 'redeem' those lands inhabited by Italians but not included within the Italian state (principally Trieste, Trentino, south Tyrol, Istria and Fiume).

Kriegschuldfrage Literally, the 'war guilt question'. Following the signing of the Treaty of Versailles, in which it was formally asserted that Germany and her allies were responsible for the war, historians and others began to question the assertion which led to revisionism and a vigorous debate over the question of war guilt.

Magyars Native name for the inhabitants of Hungary. Those who spoke Magyar were actually a minority in the Hungary that was created by the *Ausgleich* of 1867.

neue Kurs Literally, the 'new course'. When Wilhelm II became emperor of Germany in 1888 he was determined to make his mark on foreign policy, which led to Bismarck's dismissal in 1890. When the new chancellor, Caprivi, advised against renewing the Reinsurance Treaty with Russia, Wilhelm agreed, signifying that Germany was no longer dependent on Russian friendship – an essential element of Bismarck's policy.

Nihilism   A radical revolutionary movement that arose in late nineteenth-century Russia, inspired by the teachings of Mikhail Bakunin. Nihilists proclaimed their rejection of all traditional values, particularly those concerning the family and Christianity, and sought to destroy the authority of the state through terror and assassination.

'Open door'   The phrase that US secretary of state John Hay gave to his policy in China in 1899. Fearing the partition of China or that European empires would erect barriers to trade in their spheres of influence, Hay issued notes calling for all states to receive equal treatment. He claimed that there was agreement with his principle.

Plan 17   The French war plan of 1911 inspired by General Joffre's belief that the 'spirit of the offensive' was a key to victory. Rather than standing on the defensive and resisting a German attack, the French army was to seize the initiative and attack Germany.

Plan B   The Russian strategic plan for responding to a war with Germany. Based on the Franco-Russian alliance, the Russians were to go on to the offensive in the east, attacking through Poland in order to relieve pressure on the French.

Quai d'Orsay   The location of the French ministry of foreign affairs. Often used by historians as a short-hand reference to the ministry in the same way that British historians will refer to 'Whitehall' for the British government or American historians to the 'White House' for the US presidency.

Rapprochement   A term used in diplomacy and in diplomatic history to describe the re-establishment of harmonious relations between two states, usually after a crisis or a prolonged period of antagonism.

Realism   A term that is used in contrast to 'idealism'. When used in diplomacy or in diplomatic history it usually means that individual decision-makers deliberately reject ideology and sentiment in favour of measurable objectives and interests.

Reichsrat   The Austrian Chamber of Deputies, or parliament, established in Vienna in 1907. Based on universal male suffrage, the chamber was relatively powerless as the ministers were not responsible to it.

Reichstag   The German parliament that was established in Berlin by the constitution of 1871. It was based on universal manhood suffrage and it could block certain measures, but it could not initiate legislation. Ministers did not need to be appointed from it, nor were they responsible to it.

Revanche   Literally, 'revenge'. In diplomatic history, the term refers to the desire of the French, after 1871, to avenge their defeat in the Franco-Prussian War. The movement usually focused on the recovery of the 'lost provinces' of Alsace and Lorraine that were taken from France by the Treaty of Frankfurt.

Risorgimento   Literally, 'resurrection'. Used by Camillo Cavour as the title of the Piedmontese newspaper (*Il Risorgimento*) that he founded in 1847 with the aim of promoting the unification of all Italian-speaking peoples. Now used by historians to refer to the Italian unification movement generally.

Schlieffen plan   Devised by count Alfred von Schlieffen, chief of the Prussian general staff, 1891–1905. Designed in 1895 as a strategic response to the prospect of a two-front war following the formation of the Franco-Russian alliance, the plan was to knock out France quickly by invading through Holland, Belgium and Luxembourg. Although modified, the basic premise remained when Germany attacked through Belgium in 1914.

Slavophilia   A term used to describe the movement in Russia that rejected the policy of westernisation that had first been launched by Peter the Great. Popular with many Russian intellectuals in the mid-nineteenth century, the movement led later in the century to a concentration on unifying all Slavic peoples, i.e. 'panslavism'.

Theocracy   A form of government based on the rule of God, in which the laws of the state are those prescribed by religious doctrine or interpretation of the deity's will.

Weltpolitik   Literally, 'world policy'. The term is used to describe the policies of the government of Wilhelm II in which Germany was to take its place as one of the great powers of the world. The policy led to the building of a high-seas fleet and to attempts to gain colonial territories, particularly in Africa and the far east.

BIBLIOGRAPHY

COLLECTIONS OF DOCUMENTS

1 *auswärtige Politik Serbiens, Die: 1903–14*, M. Bogitschewitsch (ed.), 3 vols, Berlin, 1928–31.
2 *British Documents on the Origins of the War*, G.P. Gooch and H. Temperley (eds), 11 vols, London, 1927–38.
3 *documenti diplomatici italiani, I: 1861–1914*, 4th and 5th series, A. Torre (ed.), Rome, 1954, 1964.
4 *Documents Diplomatiques Françaises: 1871–1914*, 2^e Serie, Paris, 1930–35, 3^e Serie, Paris, 1929–36.
5 *German Diplomatic Documents: 1871–1914*, E.T.S. Dugdale, (ed. and trans.), 4 vols, London and New York, 1928.
6 *Grosse Politik der Europäischen Kabinette: 1871–1914*, J. Lepsius, A. Mendellsohn-Bartholdy and F. Thimme (eds), 39 vols, Berlin, 1922.
7 Geiss, I., *July 1914: The Outbreak of the First World War. Selected Documents*, New York, 1968.
8 *Österreich-Ungarns Aussenpolitik von der Bosnischen Krise 1908 bis zum Kriegsausbruch 1914*, L. Bittner, A. Pribram, H. Srbik and H. Uebersberger (eds), 8 vols, Vienna, 1930.

AUTOBIOGRAPHIES, MEMOIRS AND DIARIES

9 Agathon, *Les jeunes gens d'aujourd'hui*, Paris, 1913.
10 Abrikossow, D.I., *Revelations of a Russian Diplomat*, Seattle, Wash., 1964.
11 Asquith, H.H., *Genesis of the War*, London, 1923.
12 Barthélemy, J., *Démocratie et politique étrangère*, Paris, 1917.
13 Basily, N. de, *Diplomat of Imperial Russia*, Stanford, Calif., 1973.
14 Bismarck, O. von, *Die gesammelten Werke* (ed. H. von Petersdorff et al.), 15 vols, Berlin, 1923–33.
15 Bogitshevich, M., *The Causes of the War*, London, 1920.
16 Bülow, B. von, *Memoirs*, 4 vols, trans. F.A. Voigt, New York, 1930–32.
17 Caillaux, J., *Mes mémoires*, 3 vols, Paris, 1942–47.
18 Cambon, J., *The Diplomat*, London, 1931.

19   Cambon, P., *Correspondance 1870–1914*, ed. H. Cambon, 3 vols, Paris, 1940–46.
20   Chirol, V., *Fifty Years in a Changing World*, London, 1927.
21   Churchill, W. S., *The World Crisis 1911–18*, 2 vols, London, 1968.
22   Conrad von Hoetzendorf, Count F., *Aus meiner Dienstzeit*, 4 vols, Vienna, 1921.
23   Ebel, G. (ed.), *Botschafter Paul Graf von Hatzfeldt Nachgelassene Papiere 1838–1901*, 2 vols, Boppard, 1976.
24   Eckardstein, H. von, *Lebenserinnerungen und Politische Denkwürdigkeiten*, 3 vols, Leipzig, 1919–21.
25   Erdmann, K.D. (ed.), *Kurt Riezler: Tagebücher, Aufsätze, Dokumente*, Göttingen, 1972.
26   Fellner, F. (ed.), *Das politische Tagebüch Josef Redlichs*, Vienna, 1953.
27   George, D. Lloyd, *The War Memoirs of David Lloyd George*, 6 vols, London, 1933–36.
28   Gérard, A., *Mémoires d'Auguste Gérard*, Paris, 1928.
29   Giers, N.K., *The Education of a Russian Statesman*, (eds C. and B. Jelavich), Stanford, Calif., 1962.
30   Giolitti, G., *Memoirs of My Life*, London, 1923.
31   Grant, N.F., *The Kaiser's Letters to the Tsar*, London, 1920.
32   Grey, E., *Twenty-five Years 1892–1916*, 2 vols, London, 1925.
33   Haldane, R.B., *Before the War*, London, 1920.
34   Hardinge of Penshurst, Lord, *Old Diplomacy*, London, 1947.
35   Isvolsky, A.P., *The Memoirs of Alexander Iswolski*, Academic International, Tallahasee, Fl., 1974.
36   Kalmykov, A.D., *Memoirs of a Russian Diplomat*, New Haven, Conn., 1971.
37   Kokovtsov, V.N., *Out of My Past*, Stanford, Calif., 1935.
38   Lichnowsky, Prince, *My Mission to London*, London, 1918.
39   Loreburn, Lord, *How the War Came*, London, 1919.
40   Messimy, A., *Mes souvenirs*, Paris, 1937.
41   Morley, J., *Memorandum on Resignation, August 1914*, London, 1928.
42   Neklyudov, A.V., *Diplomatic Reminiscences*, London, 1920.
43   Paléologue, M., *An Ambassador's Memoirs*, 3 vols, London, 1923–25.
44   Paléologue, M., *The Turning Point: Three Critical Years, 1904–06*, London, 1935.
45   Poincaré, R., *The Origins of the War*, London, 1922.
46   Poincaré, R., *Memoirs*, 4 vols, London, 1926–30.
47   Przibram, L. Ritter von, *Erinnerungen eines alten Oesterreichers*, 2 vols, Stuttgart, 1912.
48   Redlich, J. (ed.), *J.M. Baernreither: Fragmente eines politischen Tagebuchs*, Berlin, 1928.
49   Rich, N. and M.H. Fisher (eds), *The Holstein Papers*, 4 vols, Cambridge, 1955–63.

50   Ringhoffer, K. (ed.), *The Bernstorff Papers*, 2 vols, London, 1908.
51   Rosen, Baron R.R., *Forty Years of Diplomacy*, 2 vols, London, 1922.
52   Saint Aulare, Comte de, *Confession d'un vieux diplomate*, Paris, 1953.
53   Salandra, A., *Italy and the Great War, from Neutrality to Intervention*, London, 1932.
54   Sazonov, S.D., *Fateful Years 1909–16*, London, 1928.
55   Schebeko, N., *Souvenirs*, Paris, 1936.
56   Schmoller, G. von, *Zwanzig Jahre deutscher Politik 1897–1917*, Munich and Leipzig, 1920.
57   Sonnino, S., *Diario* (eds B.F. Brown and P. Pastorelli), 3 vols, Bari, 1972.
58   Tirpitz, A. von, *My Memoirs*, 2 vols, London, 1919.
59   Tittoni, T., *Italy's Foreign and Colonial Policy*, London, 1915.
60   Varé, D., *Laughing Diplomat*, London, 1938.

GENERAL BOOKS

61   Adams, M.C.C., *The Great Adventure: Male Desire and the Coming of World War I*, Bloomington, Ind., 1990.
62   Albertini, L., *The Origins of the War of 1914*, 3 vols, London, 1952–57.
63   Allain, J.-C., *Agadir 1911, une crise impérialiste en Europe pour la conquête du Maroc*, Paris, 1976.
64   Anderson, E.N., *The First Moroccan Crisis, 1904–06*, Chicago, Ill., 1930.
65   Anderson, M.S., *The Eastern Question*, London, 1966.
66   Barlow, I.C., *The Agadir Crisis*, Durham, N.C., 1940.
67   Barnes, H.E., *The Genesis of the World War: An Introduction to the Problem of War Guilt*, New York, 1927.
68   Bayer, T.A., *England und der neue Kurs, 1890–95*, Tübingen, 1955.
69   Bridge, F.R., *Great Britain and Austria-Hungary, 1906–14*, London, 1972.
70   Bridge, F.R. and R. Bullen, *The Great Powers and the European States System, 1815–1914*, London, 1980.
71   Carlgren, W.M., *Iswolsky und Aehrenthal vor der bosnischen Annexionskrise*, Uppsala, 1955.
72   Churchill, R.P., *The Anglo-Russian Convention of 1907*, Cedar Rapids, Iowa, 1939.
73   Crampton, R.J., *The Hollow Detente: Anglo-German Relations in the Balkans, 1911–14*, London, 1980.
74   Decleva, E., *Da Adua a Sarajevo. La Politica estera italiana e la Francia 1896–1914*, Bari, 1971.
75   Dedijer, V., *The Road to Sarajevo*, London, 1967.
76   Droz, J., *Les causes de la première guerre mondiale: essai d'historiographie*, Paris, 1973.

77 Earle, E.M., *Turkey, the Great Powers and the Baghdad Railway*, New York, 1923.
78 Evans, R.J.W. and H. Pogge van Strandmann (eds), *The Coming of the First World War*, Oxford, 1988.
79 Fay, S.B., *The Origins of the World War*, 2 vols, New York, 1928.
80 Gillard, D., *The Struggle for Asia 1828–1914: A Study in British and Russian Imperialism*, London, 1977.
81 Hale, O.J., *Publicity and Diplomacy: With Special Reference to England and Germany, 1890–1914*, New York, 1940.
82 Halpern, P., *The Mediterranean Naval Situation, 1908–14*, Cambridge, Mass., 1971.
83 Helmreich, E.C., *The Diplomacy of the Balkan Wars*, Cambridge, Mass., 1938.
84 Hinsley, F.H., *Power and the Pursuit of Peace*, Cambridge, 1963.
85 Holsti, K., *Peace and War: Armed Conflict and International Order, 1648–1989*, New York, 1991.
86 Howard, H. N., *The Partition of Turkey: A Diplomatic History, 1913–23*, New York, 1966.
87 Joll, J., *The Unspoken Assumptions*, London, 1968.
88 Joll, J., *The Origins of the First World War*, London, 1984.
89 Kennedy, P.M. (ed.), *The War Plans of the Great Powers 1880–1914*, London, 1979.
90 Koch, H.W. (ed.), *The Origins of the First World War: Great Power Rivalry and War Aims*, London, 1972.
91 Langer, W.L., *European Alliances and Alignments, 1871–90*, New York, 1950.
92 Langhorne, R.T.B., *The Collapse of the Concert of Europe: International Politics, 1890–1914*, London, 1981.
93 Lee, D.E., *Europe's Crucial Years: The Diplomatic Background of World War I, 1902–1914*, Hanover, N.H., 1974.
94 May, E.R. (ed.), *Knowing One's Enemies: Intelligence Assessment Before the Two World Wars*, Princeton, N.J., 1984.
95 Millett, A.R. and W. Murray (eds), *Military Effectiveness*, Vol. 1, *The First World War*, Boston, Mass., 1988.
96 Milner, S., *The Dilemmas of Internationalism: French Syndicalism and the International Labour Movement, 1900–1914*, New York, 1990.
97 Mosse, W.E., *The European Powers and the German Question, 1848–1871*, Cambridge, 1958.
98 Nish, I., *The Anglo-Japanese Alliance: The Diplomacy of Two Island Empires, 1894–1907*, London, 1977.
99 Offer, A., *The First World War: An Agrarian Interpretation*, Oxford, 1989.
100 Petrovich, M.B., *A History of Modern Serbia*, 2 vols, New York, 1976.
101 Poidevin, R., *Les origines de la première guerre mondiale*, Paris, 1975.

102   Poidevin, R. and J. Bariety, *Les relations franco-allemandes,*
      1815–1975, Paris, 1977.
103   Remak, J. (ed.), *The Origins of World War I, 1870–1914*, New
      York, 1967.
104   Renouvin, P., *La Crise européene et la Première Guerre Mondiale*,
      Paris, 1962.
105   Rock, S.R., *Why Peace Breaks Out: Great Power Rapprochement in*
      Historical Perspective, Chapel Hill, N.C., 1989.
106   Röhl, J.C.G., *1914: Delusion or Design? The Testimony of Two*
      German Diplomats, London, 1973.
107   Rolo, P.J.V., *Entente Cordiale: The Origins and Negotiation of the*
      Anglo-French Agreements of 8 April 1904, London, 1969.
108   Salvatorelli, L., *La triplice alleanza, storia diplomatica*, Milan, 1939.
109   Schmitt, B.E., *The Coming of the War, 1914*, 2 vols, New York, 1930.
110   Taylor, A.J.P., *The Struggle for Mastery in Europe, 1848–1914*,
      Oxford, 1954.
111   Taylor, A.J.P., *War by Time-table: How the First World War Began*,
      London, 1969.
112   Turner, L.C.F., *Origins of the First World War*, London, 1970.
113   White, J.A., *The Diplomacy of the Russo-Japanese War*, Princeton,
      N.J., 1965.
114   Williamson, S., *The Politics of Grand Strategy: Britain and France*
      Prepare for War, 1904–14, Cambridge, Mass., 1969.

GENERAL ARTICLES

115   Andrew, C.M., 'German world policy and the reshaping of the Dual
      Alliance', *Journal of Contemporary History*, I (1966).
116   Andrew, C.M., 'The Entente Cordiale from its origins to 1914', in N.
      Waites (ed.), *Troubled Neighbours: Franco-British Relations in The*
      Twentieth Century, London, 1971.
117   Askew, W.C, 'The Austro-Italian antagonism, 1896–1914', in L.P.
      Wallace and W.C. Askew (eds), *Power, Public Opinion and*
      Diplomacy, Durham, N.C., 1959.
118   Barker, N.N., 'Austria, France, and the Venetian question, 1861–66',
      Journal of Modern History, XXXVI (1964).
119   Bovykin, V.I., 'The Franco-Russian alliance', *History*, LXIV (1979).
120   Cook, K.S., 'Russia, Austria, and the question of Italy, 1859–1862',
      International History Review, II (1980).
121   Corrigan, H.S.W., 'German-Turkish relations and the outbreak of
      war in 1914: a reassessment', *Past & Present*, xxxvi (1967).
122   Dakin, D., 'The diplomacy of the great powers and the Balkan states,
      1908–1914', *Balkan Studies*, III (1962).
123   Davis, H.W.C., 'The genesis of the war', *English Historical Review*,
      XXXIX (1924).

124   Edwards, E.W., 'The Japanese alliance and the Anglo-French agreement of 1904', *History*, XLII (1957).

125   Edwards, E.W., 'The Franco-German agreement on Morocco, 1909', *English Historical Review*, LXXVIII (1963).

126   Evans, E.L. and J.O. Baylen, 'History as propaganda: the German Foreign Office and the "Enlightenment" of American historians on the war guilt question', *Canadian Journal of History*, X (1975).

127   Farrar, L.L., 'Importance of omnipotence: the paralysis of the European great power system, 1871–1914', *International Review of History and Political Science*, IX (1972).

128   Fay, S.B., 'The Kaiser's secret negotiations with the tsar, 1904–1905', *American Historical Review*, XXIV (1918).

129   Gordon, M.R., 'Domestic conflict and the origins of the First World War: the British and the German cases', *Journal of Modern History*, XLVI (1974).

130   Fuller, J.V., 'The war-scare of 1875', *American Historical Review*, XXIV (1919).

131   Gauld, W.A., 'The *Dreikaiserbündnis* and the Eastern question, 1871–6', *English Historical Review*, XL (1925).

132   Gauld, W.A., 'The "Dreikaiserbündnis" and the Eastern question, 1877–8', *English Historical Review*, XLII (1927).

133   Geiss, I., 'The outbreak of the First World War and German war aims', *Journal of Contemporary History*, I (1966).

134   Greaves, R.L., 'Some aspects of the Anglo-Russian convention and its working in Persia, 1907–14', *Bulletin of the School of Oriental and African Studies*, XXXI (1968).

135   Guillen, P.G., 'Les questions coloniales dans les relations franco-allemandes à la veille de la première guerre mondiale', *La Revue Historique*, (1972).

136   Hargreaves, J.D., 'The origins of the Anglo-French military conversations in 1905', *History*, XXXVI (1951).

137   Hatton, P.H.S., 'The First World War: Britain and Germany in 1914, the July crisis and war aims', *Past & Present*, xxxvi (1967).

138   Hatton, P.H.S., 'Harcourt and Solf: the search for an Anglo-German understanding through Africa 1912–14', *European Studies Review*, I (1971).

139   Helmreich, J.E., 'Belgian concern over neutrality and British intentions, 1906–14', *Journal of Modern History*, XXXVI (1964).

140   Hering, G., 'Die serbisch bulgarische Beziehungen am Vorabend der Balkan kreige', *Balkan Studies*, III (1962).

141   Herwig, H.H., 'Clio deceived: patriotic self-censorship in Germany after the Great War', *International Security*, XII (1987).

142   Hillgruber, A., 'Die "Krieg-in-sicht" – krise 1875', in E. Schulin (ed.), *Gedenkschrift Martin Gohring, Studien zur europäischen Geschichte*, Wiesbaden, 1968.

143   Hinsley, F.H., 'Bismarck, Salisbury and the Mediterranean agreements of 1887', *Historical Journal*, I (1958).

144   Jelavich, B., 'Romania in the First World War: the pre-war crisis, 1912–1914', *International History Review*, XIV (1992).

145   Joll, J., 'The 1914 debate continues. Fritz Fischer and his critics', *Past & Present*, xxxiv (1966).

146   Joll, J., 'Politicians and the freedom to choose: the case of July 1914', in A. Ryan (ed.), *The Idea of Freedom, Essays in Honour of Isaiah Berlin*, Oxford, 1979.

147   Kann, R.A., 'Dynastic relations and European power politics (1848–1918)', *Journal of Modern History*, XXXXV (1973).

148   Koch, H.W., 'The Anglo-German alliance negotiations, missed opportunity or myth', *History*, LIV (1969).

149   Long, J., 'Franco-Russian relations during the Russo-Japanese war', *Slavonic and East European Review*, LII (1974).

150   Martel, G., 'Generals die in bed: modern warfare and modernist culture', *Journal of Canadian Studies*, XVI (1981).

151   Martel, G., 'Toynbee, McNeill and the myth of world history', *International History Review*, XII (1990).

152   Mayer, A.J., 'Domestic origins of the First World War', in L. Krieger and F. Stern (eds), *The Responsibility of Power*, New York, 1967.

153   Mayer, S.L., 'Anglo-German rivalry at the Algeçiras Conference', in P. Gifford and W.R. Louis (eds), *Britain and Germany in Africa*, New Haven, Conn., 1967.

154   Mosse, W.E., 'The end of the Crimean system: England, Russia and the neutrality of the Black Sea, 1870–1', *Historical Journal*, IV (1961).

155   Oppel, B.F., 'The waning of a traditional alliance: Russia and Germany after the Portsmouth peace conference', *Central European History*, V (1972).

156   Prevelakis, Elentherios, 'Elentherios Venizelos and the Balkan wars', *Balkan Studies*, VII (1966).

157   Remak, J., '1914 – the Third Balkan War: origins reconsidered', *Journal of Modern History*, XLIII (1971).

158   Schroeder, P.W., 'World War I as "Galloping Gertie": a reply to Joachim Remak', *Journal of Modern History*, XLIV (1972).

159   Schmitt, B.E., 'Triple Alliance and Triple Entente, 1902–1914', *American Historical Review*, XXIX (1924).

160   Steinberg, J., 'Diplomatie als Wille und Vorstellung: Die Berliner Mission Lord Haldanes in Februar 1912', in H. Schottelius and W. Deist (eds), *Marine und Marinepolitik im kaiserlichen Deutschland 1871–1914*, Düsseldorf, 1972.

161   Stone, N., 'Moltke-Conrad: relations between the Austro-Hungarian and German general staffs, 1909–14', *Historical Journal*, IX (1966).

162   Sweet, D.W., 'The Bosnian crisis', in F.H. Hinsley (ed.), *British Foreign Policy under Sir Edward Grey*, Cambridge, 1977.

163 Turner, L.C.F., 'The role of the general staffs in July 1914',
     Australian Journal of Politics and History, XIII (1965).
164 Valiani, L., 'Italian-Austro-Hungarian negotiations, 1914–15',
     Journal of Contemporary History, I (1966).
165 Williams, B.J., 'The strategic background to the Anglo-Russian
     entente of August 1907', *Historical Journal*, IX (1966).
166 Wilson, K.M., 'The Agadir crisis, the Mansion House speech and the
     double-edgedness of agreements', *Historical Journal*, XV (1972).
167 Xantalos, D., 'The Greeks and the Turks on the eve of the Balkan
     wars', *Balkan Studies*, III (1962).

GERMANY

Books

168 Berghahn, V.R., *Der Tirpitz Plan: Genesis und Verfall einer
     innenpolitische Krisenstrategie unter Wilhelm II*, Düsseldorf, 1971.
169 Berghahn, V.R., *Germany and the Approach of War in 1914*,
     London, 1973.
170 Calleo, D., *The German Problem Reconsidered*, Cambridge, 1978.
171 Craig, G.A., *Germany, 1866–1945*, Oxford, 1978.
172 Dehio, L., *Germany and World Politics in the Twentieth Century*,
     New York, 1959.
173 Deist, W., *Flottenpolitik und Flottenpropaganda*, Stuttgart, 1976.
174 Eyck, E., *Bismarck and the German Empire*, London, 1968.
175 Farrar Jr., L.L., *The Short-War Illusion: German Policy, Strategy and
     Domestic Affairs August–December 1914*, Oxford, 1973.
176 Fischer, F., *Germany's Aims in the First World War*, London, 1967.
177 Fischer, F., *War of Illusions*, London, 1975.
178 Geiss, I., *German Foreign Policy, 1871–1914*, London, 1976.
179 Guillen, P., *L'Allemagne et le Maroc de 1870 à 1905*, Paris, 1967.
180 Hauser, O., *Deutschland und der englisch-russische Gegensatz,
     1900–14*, Göttingen, 1958.
181 Hillgruber, A., *Bismarcks Aussenpolitik*, Freiburg, 1972.
182 Jarausch, K.H., *The Enigmatic Chancellor*, New Haven, Conn., 1973.
183 Kitchen, M., *The German Officer Corps, 1890–1914*, Oxford, 1968.
184 Messerschmidt, M., *Militar und Politik in der Bismarckzeit und im
     Wilhelminischen Deutschland*, Darmstadt, 1975.
185 Moritz, A., *Das Problem des Praventivkrieges in der deutschen
     Politik wahrend der ersten Marokkokrise*, Frankfurt A.M., 1974.
186 Nicholls, A.J., *Germany after Bismarck: The Caprivi Era, 1890–94*,
     New York, 1968 edn.
187 Rich, N., *Friedrich von Holstein: Politics and Diplomacy in the Era
     of Bismarck and Wilhelm II*, 2 vols, Cambridge, 1965.
188 Ritter, G., *The Schlieffen Plan: Critique of a Myth*, Westport, Conn.,
     1979.

189   Schottelius, H. and W. Deist (eds), *Marine und Marinepolitik im Kaiserlichen Deutschland, 1871–1914*, Dusseldorf, 1972.
190   Smith, W.D., *The German Colonial Empire*, Chapel Hill, N.C., 1978.
191   Steinberg, J., *Yesterday's Deterrent: Tirpitz and the Birth of the German Battlefleet*, London, 1965.
192   Thompson, W.C., *In the Eye of the Storm: Kurt Riezler and the Crises of Modern Germany*, Iowa City, Iowa, 1980.
193   Trumpener, U., *Germany and the Ottoman Empire, 1914–18*, Princeton, N.J., 1968.
194   Vogel, B., *Deutsche Russlandpolitik 1900–06*, Düsseldorf, 1973.
195   Winzen, P., *Bülow's Weltmachtkonzept*, Boppard A.R., 1977.

Articles

196   Austensen, R.A., 'Austria and the "Struggle for Supremacy in Germany"', 1848–1864', *Journal of Modern History*, LII (1980).
197   Barkin, K.D., 'Conflict and concord in Wilhelmian social thought', *Central European History*, V (1972).
198   Chickering, R., 'Patriotic societies and German foreign policy, 1890–1914', *International History Review*, I (1979).
199   Crampton, R.J., 'The Balkans as a factor in German foreign policy, 1911–1914', *Slavonic and East European Review*, LV (1977).
200   Eley, G., 'Sammlungspolitik, social imperialism and the Navy Law of 1898', *Militärgeschichtliche Mitteilungen*, I (1974).
201   Eley, G., 'Reshaping the Right: radical nationalism and the German Navy League, 1898–1908', *Historical Journal*, XXI (1978).
202   Eley, G., 'Bismarckian Germany', in G. Martel (ed.), *Modern Germany Reconsidered, 1870–1945*, London, 1991.
203   Ganz, A.H., 'The German navy in the Far East and Pacific: the seizure of Kiatschow and after', in J. Moses and P.M. Kennedy (eds), *Germany in the Pacific and Far East 1870–1914*, St Lucia, Queensland, 1977.
204   Herwig, H.H., 'Industry, Empire and the First World War', in G. Martel (ed.), *Modern Germany Reconsidered, 1870–1945*, London, 1991.
205   Jarausch, K.H., 'The illusion of limited war: Chancellor Bethmann Hollweg's calculated risk, July 1914', *Central European History*, II (1969).
206   Kaiser, D.E., 'Germany and the origins of the First World War', *Journal of Modern History*, LV (1983).
207   Kaminski, T.M., 'Bismarck and the Polish question: the "Huldingungsfahrten" to Varzin in 1894', *Canadian Journal of History*, XXIII (1988).
208   Kennedy, P.M., 'Tirpitz, England and the second Navy Law of 1900: a strategical critique', *Militärgeschichtliche Mitteilungen*, II (1970).
209   Kennedy, P.M., 'German world policy and the alliance negotiations

with England, 1897–1900', *Journal of Modern History*, XLV (1973).

210 Kennedy, P.M., 'The development of German naval operations plans against England, 1896–1914', *English Historical Review*, LXXXIX (1974).

211 Mortimer, J.S., 'Commercial interests and German diplomacy in the Agadir crisis', *Historical Journal*, X (1967).

212 Röhl, J.C.G., 'Admiral von Müller and the approach of war, 1911–1914', *Historical Journal*, XII (1969).

213 Showalter, D.E., 'Army and society in Imperial Germany: the pains of modernization', *Journal of Contemporary History*, XVIII (1983).

214 Steinberg, J., 'The Copenhagen complex', *Journal of Contemporary History*, I (1966).

215 Steinberg, J., 'The novella of 1908: necessities and choices in the Anglo-German naval arms race', *Transactions of the Royal Historical Society*, 5th ser., xxi (1971).

216 Stern, F., 'Bethmann Hollweg and the war: the limits of responsibility', in L. Krieger and F. Stern (eds), *The Responsibility of Power*, Garden City, N.Y., 1967.

217 Stern, F., 'German historians and the war: Fritz Fischer and his critics', in F. Stern (ed.), *The Failure of Illiberalism: Essays on the Political Culture of Modern Germany*, New York, 1972.

218 Trumpener, U., 'Liman von Sanders and the German Ottoman alliance', *Journal of Contemporary History*, I (1966).

219 Turner, L.C.F., 'The significance of the Schlieffen plan', *Australian Journal of Politics and History*, xiii (1967).

AUSTRIA-HUNGARY

Books

220 Bridge, F.R., *From Sadowa to Sarajevo*, London, 1972.

221 Deak, I., *Beyond Nationalism: A Social and Political History of the Habsburg Officer Corps, 1848–1918*, New York, 1990.

222 Hantsch, H., *Leopold, Graf Berchtold*, 2 vols, Graz, 1963.

223 Lafore, L., *The Long Fuse*, London, 1966.

224 Macartney, C.A., *The Habsburg Monarchy, 1790–1918*, London, 1968.

225 May, A.J., *The Hapsburg Monarchy, 1867–1914*, Cambridge, Mass., 1965.

226 Pribram, A., *Austrian Foreign Policy, 1908–18*, London, 1923.

227 Rothenberg, G.E., *The Army of Francis Joseph*, West Lafayette, Ind., 1976.

228 Williamson Jr., S.R., *Austria-Hungary and the Origins of the First World War*, London, 1994.

Articles

229 Bradley, J.F.N., 'Czech pan-Slavism before the First World War', *Slavonic and East European Review*, XL (1961).

230 Bridge, F.R., 'Tarde venientibus ossa: Austro-Hungarian colonial aspirations in Asia Minor, 1913–14', *Middle Eastern Studies*, (1970).

231 Bridge, F.R., 'Izvolsky, Aehrenthal and the end of the Austro-Russian entente, 1906–08', *Mitteilungen des österreichischen Staatsarchivs*, XXIX (1976).

232 Bridge, F.R., 'Austria-Hungary and the Balkan states, 1906–1908', in F.H. Hinsley (ed.), *British Foreign Policy under Sir Edward Grey*, Cambridge, 1977.

233 Fellner, F., 'Die Haltung Oesterreich-Ungarns wahrend der Konferenz von Algeciras, 1906', *Mitteilungen des Instituts fur österreichische Geschichtsforschung*, LXXI (1963).

234 Jannen Jr., W., 'The Austro-Hungarian decision for war in July 1914', in S.R. Williamson Jr. and P. Pastor (eds), *Essays on World War I: Origins and Prisoners of War*, New York, 1983.

235 Kraehe, E.E., 'Austria and the problem of reform in the German Confederation, 1851–1863', *American Historical Review*, LVI (1951).

236 Peterson, M.B.A., 'Das österreichischen-ungarische Memorandum an Deutschland vom 5 July 1914', *Scandia*, 30 (1964).

237 Stone, N., 'Hungary and the crisis of July 1914', *Journal of Contemporary History*, I (1966).

238 Turczynski, E., 'Österreich-Ungarn und Sudosteuropa wahrend der Balkan kriege', *Balkan Studies*, V (1964).

239 Wank, S., 'Aehrenthal and the Sanjak railway project: a reappraisal', *Slavonic and East European Review*, XLII (1964).

240 Williamson Jr., S.R., 'Vienna and July 1914: the origins of the Great War once more', in S.R. Williamson Jr. and P. Pastor (eds), *Essays on World War I: Origins and Prisoners of War*, New York, 1983.

ITALY

Books

241 Askew, W.C., *Europe and Italy's Acquisition of Libya, 1911–12*, Durham, N.C., 1959.

242 Blumberg, A., *A Carefully Planned Accident: The Italian War of 1859*, Selingsgrove, N.J., 1990.

243 Bosworth, R.J.B., *Italy, the Least of the Great Powers: Italian foreign policy before the First World War*, New York, 1979.

244 Bosworth, R.J.B., *Italy and the Approach of the First World War*, London, 1983.

245 Coppa, F.J., *Planning, Protectionism and Politics in Liberal Italy: Economics and Politics in the Giolittian Age*, Washington, D.C., 1971.
246 Drake, R., *Byzantium for Rome: The Politics of Nostalgia in Umbertian Italy, 1878–1900*, Chapel Hill, N.C., 1980.
247 Glanville, J.L., *Italy's Relations with England, 1896–1905*, Baltimore, Md., 1934.
248 Gooch, J., *Army, State, and Society in Italy, 1870–1915*, New York, 1989.
249 Hess, R.L., *Italian Colonialism in Somalia*, Chicago, Ill., 1966.
250 Lowe, C.J. and F. Marzari, *Italian Foreign Policy, 1870–1940*, London, 1975.
251 Mack Smith, D., *Italy, A Modern History*, rev. edn, Ann Arbor, Mich., 1969.
252 Salomone, A.W., *Italy in the Giolittian Era: Italian Democracy in the Making, 1900–14*, Philadelphia, Penn., 1960.
253 Thayer, J.A., *Italy and the Great War: Politics and Culture, 1870–1915*, Madison, Wis., 1964.
254 Webster, R.A., *Industrial Imperialism in Italy, 1908–1915*, Berkeley, Calif., 1975.
255 Whittam, J., *The Politics of the Italian Army, 1861–1918*, London, 1977.

Articles

256 Cameron, R.E., 'French finance and Italian unity: the Cavourian decade', *American Historical Review*, LXII (1957)
257 Cunsolo, R.S., 'Libya, Italian nationalism and the revolt against Giolitti', *Journal of Modern History*, XXXVII (1963).
258 Haines, C.G., 'Italian Irredentism during the Near Eastern Crisis 1875–78', *Journal of Modern History*, IX (1937).
259 Hess, R.L., 'Italy and Africa: colonial ambitions in the First World War', *Journal of African History*, IV (1963).
260 Jones, S., 'Antonio Salandra and the politics of Italian intervention in the First World War', *European History Quarterly*, XV (1985).
261 Renzi, W.A., 'Italy's neutrality and entrance into the Great War: a re-examination', *American Historical Review*, LXXIII (1968).
262 Tamborra, A., 'The rise of Italian industry and the Balkans (1900–14)', *Journal of European Economic History*, III (1974).

RUSSIA

Books

263 Fuller Jr., W.C., *Civil-Military Conflict in Imperial Russia 1881–1914*, Cambridge, 1981.

264 Lieven, D.C.B., *Russia and the Origins of the First World War*, London, 1983.
265 McDonald, D.M., *United Government and Foreign Policy in Russia 1900–1914*, Cambridge, Mass., 1992.
266 Seton-Watson, R.W., *The Russian Empire, 1801–1917*, Oxford, 1967.
267 Thaden, E.C., *Conservative Nationalism in Nineteenth-century Russia*, Seattle, Wash., 1964.
268 Thaden, E.C., *Russia and the Balkan Alliance of 1912*, Philadelphia, Penn., 1965.
269 Walicki, A., *The Slavophile Controversy*, Oxford, 1975.
270 Westwood, J.N., *Endurance and Endeavour: Russian History, 1812–1980*, Oxford, 1981.

Articles

271 Bestuzhev, I.V., 'Russian foreign policy, February–June 1914', *Journal of Contemporary History*, I (1966).
272 Bushnell, J., 'The Tsarist Officer Corps, 1881–1914: customs, duties, inefficiency', *American Historical Review*, LXXXVI (1981).
273 Collins, D.N., 'The Franco-Russian alliance and Russian railways, 1891–1914', *Historical Journal*, XVI (1973).
274 Dorpalen, A., 'Tsar Alexander III and the Boulanger Crisis in France', *Journal of Modern History*, XXIII (1951).
275 Helmreich, E.C. and C.E. Black, 'The Russo-Bulgarian military convention of 1902', *Journal of Modern History*, IX (1937).
276 Hutchinson, J.F., 'The Octobrists and the future of Russia as a great power', *Slavonic and East European Review*, I (1972).
277 Jelavich, C., 'Russo-Bulgarian relations, 1892–1896: with particular reference to the problem of the Bulgarian succession', *Journal of Modern History*, XXIV (1952).
278 Johnson, R.J., 'Zagranichnaia Agentura: the Tsarist political police in Europe', *Journal of Contemporary History*, VII (1966).
279 Lieven, D., 'Pro-Germans and Russian foreign policy 1890–1914', *International History Review*, II (1980).
280 Longley, D.A., 'The Russian Social Democrats' statement to the Duma on 26 July (8 August) 1914: a new look at the evidence', *English Historical Review*, CII (1987).
281 Morrill, D.L., 'Nicholas II and the call for the first Hague Conference', *Journal of Modern History*, XLVI (1974).
282 Perrins, M., 'Russian military policy in the Far East and the 1905 Revolution in the Russian Army', *European Studies Review*, IX (1979).
283 Turner, L.C.F., 'The Russian mobilization of 1914', *Journal of Contemporary History*, III (1968).

FRANCE

Books

284 Anderson, R.D., *France, 1870-1914, Politics and Society*, London, 1977.

285 Andrew, C.M., *Théophile Delcassé and the Making of the Entente Cordiale, 1898–1905*, London, 1968.

286 Becker, J.-J., *1914, comment les Francais sont entrés dans la guerre*, Paris, 1977.

287 Bouvier, J. and R. Girault (eds), *L'impérialisme français d'avant 1914*, Paris, 1976.

288 Brunschwig, H., *French Colonialism, 1871–1914: Myths and Realities*, London, 1966.

289 Bury, J.P.T., *France, 1814–1940*, 4th edn., London, 1969.

290 Carroll, E.M., *French Public Opinion and Foreign Affairs, 1870–1914*, London, 1931.

291 Contamine, H., *La Revanche, 1871–1914*, Paris, 1957.

292 Duroselle, J.-B., *La France et les Français, 1900–1914*, Paris, 1972.

293 Eubank, K., *Paul Cambon, Master Diplomatist*, Norman, Okla., 1960.

294 Ganiage, J., *L'Expansion coloniale de la France sous la Troisième République 1871–1914*, Paris, 1968.

295 Girardet, R., *Le nationalisme français, 1871–1914*, Paris, 1966.

296 Girardet, R., *L'idée coloniale en France de 1871 à 1962*, Paris, 1972.

297 Girault, R., *Emprunts russes et investissements français en Russie, 1887–1914*, Paris, 1973.

298 Kieger, J.F.V., *France and the Origins of the First World War*, London, 1983.

299 Mitchell, A., *The German Influence in France after 1870: The Formation of the French Republic*, Chapel Hill, N.C., 1979.

300 Poidevin, R., *Finances et relations internationales, 1887–1914*, Paris, 1970.

301 Porch, D., *The March to the Marne: The French Army 1871–1914*, New York, 1981.

302 Thobie, J., *Intérêts et impérialisme français dans l'empire Ottoman, 1895–1914*, Paris, 1977.

303 Weber, E., *The Nationalist Revival in France, 1905–1914*, Berkeley, Calif., 1959.

Articles

304 Allain, J.-C., 'L'expansion française au Maroc de 1902 à 1912', in J. Bouvier and R. Girault (eds), *L'impérialisme français d'avant 1914*, Paris, 1976.

305 Andrew, C.M., 'The French colonialist movement during the Third Republic: the unofficial mind of imperialism', *Transactions of the Royal Historical Society*, 5th ser., xxvi (1976).

306 Andrew, C.M. and A.S. Kanya-Forstner, 'The French "Colonial Party": its composition, aims and influence, 1885–1914', *Historical Journal*, XIV (1971).

307 Andrew, C.M. and A.S. Kanya-Forstner, 'The Groupe Colonial in the French Chamber of Deputies, 1892–1932', *Historical Journal*, XVII (1974).

308 Andrew, C.M. and A.S. Kanya-Forstner, 'Gabriel Hanotaux, the Colonial Party and the Fashoda strategy', *Journal of Imperial and Commonwealth History*, III (1974).

309 Cairns, J.C., 'International politics and the military mind: the case of the French Republic, 1911–14', *Journal of Modern History*, XXV (1953).

310 Cairns, J.C., 'Politics and foreign policy: the French Parliament, 1911–1914', *Canadian Historical Review*, XXXIV (1953).

311 Cooper, S.E., 'Pacifism in France, 1889–1914: international peace as a human right', *French Historical Studies*, XVII (1991).

312 Girault, R., 'Les Balkans dans les relations franco-russes en 1912', *La Revue Historique* (1975).

313 Hayne, M.B., 'The Quai d'Orsay and influences on the formulation of French foreign policy, 1898–1914', *French History*, II (1988).

314 Leaman, B.R., 'The influence of domestic policy on foreign affairs in France, 1898–1905', *Journal of Modern History*, XIV (1942).

315 Mitchell, A., ' "A Situation of Inferiority": French military reorganization after the defeat of 1870', *American Historical Review*, LXXXVI (1981).

316 Prete, R.A., 'French strategic planning and the deployment of the B.E.F. in France in 1914', *Canadian Journal of History*, XXIV (1989).

317 Prete, R.A., 'The preparation of the French Army prior to World War I: an historiographical reappraisal', *Canadian Journal of History*, XXVI (1991).

BRITAIN

Books

318 Bourne, K., *The Foreign Policy of Victorian England 1830–1902*, Oxford, 1970.

319 Busch, B.C., *Hardinge of Penshurst: A Study in the Old Diplomacy*, Hamden, Conn., 1980.

320 Busch, B.C., *Britain and the Persian Gulf, 1894–1914*, Berkeley, Calif., 1967.

321 Gooch, J., *The Plans of War: The General Staff and British Military Strategy, c. 1900–16*, Oxford, 1974.

322 Grenville, J.A.S., *Lord Salisbury and Foreign Policy: The Close of the Nineteenth Century*, London, 1964.

323 Hamilton, K., *Bertie of Thame: Edwardian Ambassador*, London, 1990.
324 Howard, C.H.D., *Splendid Isolation*, London, 1967.
325 Lowe, C.J., *Salisbury and the Mediterranean, 1886–96*, London, 1965.
326 Lowe, C.J. and M.C. Dockrill (eds), *The Mirage of Power*, 3 vols, London, 1972.
327 Marder, A.J., *British Naval Policy, 1880–1905: The Anatomy of British Sea Power*, London, 1940.
328 Martel, G., *Imperial Diplomacy: Rosebery and the Failure of Foreign Policy*, London, 1986.
329 Monger, G.W., *The End of Isolation: British Foreign Policy, 1900–1907*, Edinburgh, 1963.
330 Steiner, Z.S., *The Foreign Office and Foreign Policy, 1898–1914*, Cambridge, 1969.
331 Steiner, Z.S., *Britain and the Origins of the First World War*, London, 1977.

Articles

332 Best, G.F.A., 'Militarism and the Victorian public schools', in B. Simon and I. Bradley (eds), *The Victorian Public School*, London, 1975.
333 Bosworth, R.J.B., 'Great Britain and Italy's acquisition of the Dodecanese, 1912–1915', *Historical Journal*, XIII (1970).
334 Butterfield, H., 'Sir Edward Grey in July 1914', *Irish Historical Studies*, V (1965).
335 Chamberlain, M.E., 'Lord Cromer's "Ancient and Modern Imperialism": a proconsular view of empire', *Journal of British Studies*, XII (1972).
336 Coogan, J.W. and Peter F. Coogan, 'The British Cabinet and the Anglo-French staff talks, 1905–1914: who knew what and when did he know it?', *Journal of British Studies*, XXIV (1985).
337 Cooper, M.B., 'British policy in the Balkans, 1908–1909', *Historical Journal*, VII (1964).
338 Corp, E.T., 'Sir Eyre Crowe and the administration of the Foreign Office, 1906–1914', *Historical Journal*, XXII (1979).
339 Cosgrove, R.A., 'A note on Lloyd George's speech at the Mansion House, 21 July 1911', *Historical Journal*, XII (1966).
340 Cosgrove, R.A., 'The career of Sir Eyre Crowe: a reassessment', *Albion*, IV (1972).
341 Cowling, M., 'Lytton, the Cabinet, and the Russians, August to November 1878', *English Historical Review*, LXXVI (1961).
342 Dockrill, M.L., 'British policy during the Agadir crisis of 1911', in F.H. Hinsley (ed.), *The Foreign Policy of Sir Edward Grey*, Cambridge, 1977.

343   Douglas, R., 'Britain and the Armenian question, 1894–1897', *Historical Journal*, XIX (1976).

344   Ekstein, M., 'Sir Edward Grey and Imperial Germany in 1914', *Journal of Contemporary History*, VI (1971).

345   French, D., 'The Edwardian crisis and the origins of the First World War', *International History Review*, IV (1982).

346   Gordon, D.C., 'The Admiralty and Dominion Navies, 1902–1914', *Journal of Modern History*, XXXIII (1961).

347   Gowen, R.J., 'British Legerdemain at the 1911 Imperial Conference: the Dominions, defense planning, and the renewal of the Anglo-Japanese alliance', *Journal of Modern History*, LII (1980).

348   Grenville, J.A S., 'Lansdowne's abortive project of 12 March 1901 for a secret agreement with Germany', *Bulletin of the Institute of Historical Research*, XXVII (1954).

349   Haggie, P., 'The Royal Navy and war planning in the Fisher era', *Journal of Contemporary History*, VIII (1973).

350   Howard, C., 'MacDonald, Henderson, and the outbreak of war, 1914', *Historical Journal*, XX (1977).

351   Lammers, D., 'Arno Mayer and the British decision for war', *Journal of British Studies*, XII (1973).

352   Langhorne, R.T.B., 'The naval question in Anglo-German relations, 1912–1914', *Historical Journal*, XIV (1971).

353   Mackay, R.F., 'The Admiralty, the German navy, and the redistribution of the British fleet, 1904–1905', *Mariner's Mirror*, LVI (1970).

354   Mackintosh, J.P., 'The role of the Committee of Imperial Defence before 1914', *English Historical Review*, LXXVII (1962).

355   McDermott, J., 'The revolution in British military thinking from the Boer War to the Moroccan Crisis', *Canadian Journal of History*, XXI (1986).

356   Martel, G., 'The meaning of power: rethinking the decline and fall of Great Britain', *International History Review*, XIII (1991).

357   Meacham, S., 'The sense of an impending clash: English working-class unrest before the First World War', *American Historical Review*, LXXVII (1972).

358   Morris, A.J.A., 'The English Radicals' campaign for disarmament and the Hague Conference of 1907', *Journal of Modern History*, XLIII (1971).

359   Neilson, K., ' "My Beloved Russians": Sir Arthur Nicolson and Russia, 1906–1916', *International History Review*, IX (1987).

360   Offer, A., 'The working classes, British naval plans and the coming of the Great War', *Past & Present*, cvii (1985).

361   Preston, A., 'Frustrated great gamesmanship: Sir Garnet Wolseley's plans for war against Russia, 1873–1880', *International History Review*, II (1980).

362 Saunders, D., 'Britain and the Ukrainian question (1912–1920)', *English Historical Review*, CIII (1988).

363 Steiner, Z.S., 'Great Britain and the creation of the Anglo-Japanese alliance', *Journal of Modern History*, XXXI (1959).

364 Steiner, Z.S., 'Grey, Hardinge and the Foreign Office, 1905–10', *Historical Journal*, X (1967).

365 Watt, D.C., 'British reactions to the assassination at Sarajevo', *European Studies Review*, I (1971).

366 Wilson, K.M., 'The British cabinet's decision for war', *British Journal of International Studies*, I (1975).

367 Wilson, K.M., 'To the Western Front: British war plans and the "military entente" with France before the First World War', *British Journal of International Studies*, III (1977).

368 Wilson, T., 'Britain's "moral commitment" to France in August 1914', *History*, LXIV (1979).

MAPS

Map 1 Europe & the Mediterranean: Trouble spots & ethnic groups

Map 2 Central Europe

Map 3 East Asia

Map 4 Africa

Map 5 South-eastern Europe

▓	Germans 12 million (24%)	▒	Rumanians 3.5 million (6%)
▓	Magyars 10 million (20%)	▨	Italians 0.75 million (1.5%)
▥	Slavs 23 million (46%)		

POLAND · RUSSIA · UKRAINE · Cracow · POLES · Lemberg · Isolated POLES · RUTHENIANS · SLOVAKS · Czernowitz · Budapest · Hermannstadt · Kronstadt · R. Danube · Belgrade · RUMANIA · SERBS · SERBIA · R. Danube · SANJAK OF NOVIBAZAR · MONTENEGRO · ALBANIA

INDEX

Page numbers which appear in italics in the index refer to a short biographical description which may be found in the Guide to Characters. Page numbers which appear in bold refer to a short explanation which may be found in the Glossary.

Boulanger, General Georges, 44, 110
Boxer rebellion, 55, 114
Bridge, F. R., 9
Britain, and Austria-Hungary, 21, 29; and China, 55–6; and France, 43–5, 51, 57–9, 62–4, 71–2, 75, 83, 90; and Germany, 20–2, 46–8, 51–2, 56, 62, 65, 71–5, 83, 90; and Italy, 29, 31–2, 73; and Japan, 11, 56, 66; and Russia, 11, 36–7, 39, 50–1, 56, 58, 60, 67, 78, 82; and the July crisis, 3, 10, 82–3, 85, 89–90
Bucharest, treaty of (1913), 77
Büchlau agreement (1908), 70
Bulgaria, 7, 75–7
Bülow, Bernhard von, 11, 22, 55, 61, 63–4, 98, 110
Burns, John, 83, 111

Cambon, Paul, 63, 111
China, 42–3, 47, 54–7
Comité de l'Afrique Française, 57, 114
Committee of Imperial Defence, 74, 114
Congress of Vienna (1815), 13, 23, 28, 36, 50
Conrad von Hötzendorf, Count, 69–70, 73, 111
conscription, 5, 21
Constantinople, Treaty of (1913), 77
Crimean War (1854–56), 25–6, 34–5, 37, 50
Cromer, 1st Earl of, 60, 111
Crowe, Eyre, 62, 111
Cruppi, Jean, 71, 111
Custoza, Battle of (1866), 29

Delcassé, Théophile, 57–8, 62–3, 111
diplomatic revolution, 11, 52, 60, 68
Dogger Bank incident (1904), 60
Dreadnought, 48, 65, 114
Dreikaiserbund (*see* League of the Three Emperors)

Dual Monarch, 27–8, 69, 76, 87, 115
Dual Alliance (Austro-German), 12, 18, 29; (also *see* Franco-Russian alliance)
Duma, 66, 115

Edward VII, 58, 111
Egypt, 43, 45, 47–8, 51, 54, 57, 59
Erdmann, Karl Dietrich, 9

Fashoda crisis (1898), 42, 45, 52, 57, 65
Fay, Sidney B., 5
Ferdinand, Archduke Franz, 1–4, 111
Fichte, Johann G., 23
Fiume, 29, 31
Fischer, Fritz, 8
France, and Britain, 43–5, 51, 57–9, 62–4, 71–2, 75, 83, 90; and Germany, 13, 17, 20, 41–5, 57–8, 61–3, 71–3, 81, 84; and Italy, 29–32, 54, 64, 73; and Russia, 12–13, 33–41, 44–5, 54, 56–8, 64–5, 72, 75, 80–1, 89
Franco-German agreement on Morocco (1909), 71
Franco-Prussian War (1870–71), 12–13, 16, 38–42
Franco-Russian alliance, 12, 14, 33, 53–4, 58–9, 61, 65, 92
Frankfurt, Treaty of (1871), 13, 17, 41
Franz Joseph, 20, 38, 79, 111
Fundamental Laws (1905), 67

Garibaldi, Giuseppe, 29, 111
Geiss, Imanuel, 9
German Confederation, 23, 26–7, 115
Germany and Austria-Hungary, 10, 12, 17–18, 20–3, 26–9, 54, 64, 70, 77–81, 84–5, 87–8; and Britain 20–2, 46–8, 51–2, 56, 62, 65, 71–5, 83–90; and China, 55; and France, 13, 17, 20, 41–5, 57–8, 61–3, 71–3, 81, 84; and Italy, 12, 18, 21, 31, 82, 85; and Russia, 12, 18, 20–1, 38–9, 60–1, 63–4, 66–7,